SAFETY AT SEA

SAFETY AT SEA

A Sailor's Complete Guide to Safe Seamanship

GEORGE DAY

Illustrations by Al Barnes

G. P. Putnam's Sons   *New York*

G. P. Putnam's Sons
Publishers Since 1838
200 Madison Avenue
New York, NY 10016

Library of Congress Cataloging-in-Publication Data

Day, George, date.
    Safety at sea : a sailor's complete guide to safe seamanship / George Day ;
illustrations by Al Barnes.

        p.   cm.
    Includes index.
    1. Sailing—Safety measures.   2. Yachts and yachting—Safety
measures.   I. Title.
GV811.53.D39   1991   90-42991   CIP
797.1'246'0289—dc20
ISBN 0-399-13571-5

Printed in the United States of America

1   2   3   4   5   6   7   8   9   10

This book is printed on acid-free paper.

For the crew of *Clover*: Rosa, Simon and Timothy

CONTENTS

ACKNOWLEDGMENTS

No book is one person's creation alone. The following pages owe much to the knowledge and commitment of three people in particular: John Bonds, John Rousmaniere and Bernadette Brennan, who together are the driving forces and the consciences of the Cruising World/USYRU Safety at Sea Seminars and leaders in the important field of safety for recreational sailors and boat owners. While the thoughts, techniques and information contained in these pages will reflect some of their thinking and writing, the final work, its errors and omissions, is mine alone.

—George Day
Newport, Rhode Island
March 1990

FOREWORD

If you intend to sail offshore, you're going to like this book. Writing from a remarkable background in bluewater sailing, George Day brings to his subject outstanding technical expertise, deep consideration for one's shipmates, and an eloquence of expression which he earned through hard work and years of journeyman labor as a writer. As editor of *Cruising World*, George has been at the center of the Safety at Sea educational programs that the magazine has helped sponsor with the United States Yacht Racing Union (USYRU), drawing on programs developed at the U.S. Naval Academy. The insights drawn from ten years of those programs are an integral part of this book.

What comes through most strongly throughout these pages, however, is George Day the man. He is a remarkable fellow, philosopher by training, sailor by avocation, and writer by trade. He has taken time in his life to stop and smell the pungent aroma of salt air. He is a gentle man, thoughtful of others, reflective of habit and thorough as an experienced seaman must be. All this comes through on every page. You'll know George when you've finished, and you'll count him (as I do) a valued friend and compatriot in the congregation of the sea.

For anyone who intends to cruise with a crew of family and friends, this is essential reading.

—Captain John Bonds, U.S.N. (Ret.)
Executive Director,
United States Yacht Racing Union

INTRODUCTION: ONE HAND FOR YOURSELF

The allure of the sea is comprised of many things. We enjoy our time sailing with family and friends for the peace it brings, for the comfort away from the confines of the shore. We enjoy our coastal forays for the manageable challenges they represent, the pinprick of navigation, the careful management of wind and sail, the watchful eye on the weather and the sea. Along the coast we can serve ourselves an antidote to ordinary life by taking our fates in our own hands aboard our boats and, after an afternoon struggle with a pesky sea breeze, relax in a calm anchorage and reflect upon a job well done, a mission accomplished. There are few simple satisfactions in life that can compare.

Choosing to sail offshore is something different, although all that goes into an offshore passage stems from all that makes a great coastal run: self reliance, competent seamanship, precise navigation, good crew work and a willing, seafaring spirit. Offshore, out of sight of land and out of the ready earshot of fellow sailors and coastal working fleets, we are on our own. Of course, we are always on our own no matter where we sail. But out there, when the green coastal water turns to deep-ocean blue, the solitude is palpable. Wind and weather are met on the sea's terms. The success of a passage depends upon our ability to adapt to those terms. We must sharpen our wits and callus our palms. We have to watch the horizon with a weather eye and listen to the radio with workmanlike patience for a telling forecast.

Since sailing began, skippers have warned their crews of what lay ahead and attempted to instill in them the simple thought of what is required for a safe and satisfactory journey across the sea. They said, "One hand for the ship, lads, and one hand for yourself."

Every boy who ever set foot on a square rigger, every deck ape aboard a maxi-racer and every woman and man setting out for a cruise has heard those words. They are words to live by.

Ray Brown knew those words. He had no doubt uttered them many times to those who had sailed with him and to those who had listened to him speak at the United States Naval Academy Sailing Association's Safety at Sea Seminars. Ray was a doctor who lived in Annapolis, Maryland. He also was a sailor's sailor. That he should die at sea, while in the prime of his life, is an irony that only a cruel fate could conjure. The sea, being many things, occasionally provides that cruel fate.

Ray Brown was successful and on the verge of fulfilling a long-harbored dream of extended cruising. He had taken delivery of his new semicustom Alden 50 in Portsmouth, Rhode Island, with plans to sail south to Annapolis for the Annapolis Boat Show. The Alden was the epitome of all a seaman with Ray's experience could want in a cruising vessel. It was fitted with all the electronics he and his wife, Virginia, could need and use. It carried the latest in safety equipment. It was a thing of beauty, both functionally and aesthetically. As a showpiece for her builders and as a statement of her owner's meticulous and methodical approach to seafaring, the boat was destined to be a star of the East Coat's largest boat show.

Ray and Virginia, with their son Sayers and a crew of four others, departed Newport, Rhode Island, at midnight with a fair northerly for the 250-mile trip south to Annapolis. The crew had been briefed on safety procedures and instructed by their skipper on where safety equipment was stored and how to deploy it. Among the rules Ray laid down was one requiring that no one go forward of the cockpit during darkness except in an emergency, and then only while wearing a life harness.

Riding a fair wind, they shot south toward Block Island and Long Island. Ray stood the midnight-to-4:00 A.M. watch and then went below. They were near The Race, at Long Island's eastern end. After spending a few minutes at the chart table, Ray climbed back on deck to alter course 15 degrees. He had removed his harness while below and was ready for a well-deserved turn in his bunk.

But while on deck, something bothered him. The jib was fluttering. It was new and possibly not sheeted correctly. Ray shone a spotlight on it but needed to step forward of the cockpit to get a better look. After assessing the problem, he instructed Sayers to alter course downwind for a moment so an alteration to the sheet lead could be made. Suddenly, caught by a wave, the boat lurched, the massive main boom jibed and Ray was struck and thrown overboard.

The crew deployed the safety and man-overboard gear at hand in the cockpit. They circled quickly and returned to the spot where Ray had gone overboard. There was no sign of him. For six hours Virginia and Sayers and the crew desperately searched for their lost skipper, joined by the crews of the neighboring Coast Guard stations. Ray was never found.

A consummate seaman, Ray Brown was as methodical and knowledgeable as any sailor who frequented the mid-Atlantic and New England coasts. He had ministered medicine to thousands and taught health at sea to hundreds. Yet the sea claimed him. His passing is a tragedy that serves to remind us that no matter how much we know and how well we prepare our boats, our crews and ourselves, the sea still waits for us to make just one mistake.

ONE HAND FOR the ship and one for yourself. There have been dozens of books written for sailors on the subject of how to sail, how to buy and sell a boat, how to maintain and upgrade a sailboat. These are all worthwhile, for they add to the available knowledge that will make us better boat owners, better sailors, better navigators and better explorers of the coasts and seas.

These are books that speak to the first half of the old adage: One hand for the ship.

The chapters that follow are dedicated to the other hand, the hand you and I reserve for ourselves. The specific topic is safety and safe sailing. Sailing is unusual among pastimes and sports, for in its every aspect is the constant knowledge that the sea is capricious and on rare occasions deadly. Ray Brown knew that. Most experienced sailors do. It is the experienced sailor's ambition to appreciate the indifferent quality of the sea and by preparation, practice and planning do his utmost to overcome it. That is the challenge of coastal and offshore sailing, and meeting that challenge is its great satisfaction.

Chapter 1

PLANNING TO ARRIVE SAFELY: THE HUMAN FACTOR

SUCCESSFUL AND UNSUCCESSFUL PASSAGES

"WE HAD A wonderful trip. Dolphins. Moonlight. Fair winds." Or, "You wouldn't believe the weather. Forty knots. On the nose. Waves as tall as your house. Everyone sick. The boat a mess."

It can be the best of times. Or it can be the worst of times. Every sailing voyage seems to be an either-or experience. Almost never do you hear a bland report. The difference between a successful sailing

19

trip and one that is unsuccessful—whether a passage of 20 miles or of 2,000—is the human factor. We, as skipper and crew, have either prepared ourselves, our boat and our crew for the sail ahead, or we haven't.

The human factor is what safe sailing is all about.

My own first transoceanic cruise was aboard the Little Harbor 50 *Adele*, owned and skippered by Richard "Bunny" Burnes. *Adele* was designed by Ted Hood to be a competitive CCA racer in the 1960s. She is a wholesome boat, with plenty of displacement, a manageable yawl/ketch rig, a powerful engine and the easy lines of a true off-shore passage maker. Her skipper was and is an excellent seaman, with many transatlantic passages under his belt, as well as numerous Bermuda Races and sojourns to the Caribbean.

With a crew of seven adults, we departed Lisbon, Portugal, for a leisurely delivery trip to the Caribbean. We sailed quickly in the prevailing northerly south to Madeira and after a short stay, set off for the Canary Islands. A few items of gear, including the diesel auxiliary, gave us trouble on the first leg of the trip. But, with the ample spares aboard and a little ingenuity, we were able to repair all that broke and to carry on without pause.

The trip south to the Canary Islands should have been a sleigh ride. It wasn't. We met a stiff southerly wind and a lumpy sea that had us all green behind the ears. As we slogged on, Bunny kept spirits high with good humor, and by teaching those who had the stomach for it the art of taking a celestial sight. We arrived at Las Palmas, Grand Canary, battered but hardly bowed. We were becoming a crew, which is so much more than a simple assemblage of bodies brought together to sail a boat. No one was reluctant to make landfall. But we had tasted a small victory in our passage south, so we were all eager to get ready for the longer passage that would take us across the ocean to Barbados.

On a blazing hot November morning we hauled in the anchor in the small harbor at the island of Gomera and set sail south and west, bound for the trade winds and following on the trail Columbus had blazed some 480 years before. It is a passage made by hundreds of boats every year. But, the first time, it can have a magical aspect, for crossing an ocean takes you away from the world and binds you for a time with a small band of sailors who share your common purpose.

Our landfall in Barbados 17 days later came up right on schedule, a beautiful sight after so long at sea. A beautiful sight, as well, because we had sailed nearly 3,000 miles without serious incident, without gear breakdowns, without conflict in the crew. It was a thrilling accomplishment for those on board who were making their first ocean crossing. It was an exhilarating but somewhat routine experience for those who had sailed this way before.

That was how it was aboard *Adele*: teamwork among all the crew and clear communication from the skipper. The shipboard routine was orderly, pleasant but firm. Above all, *Adele* was prepared for the task at hand. She carried the safety equipment we might need in case of a man-overboard crisis; she had aboard the sails we would need for every wind and weather condition; her shipboard systems had been set up for passage making and had been checked and rechecked prior to departure; she carried spare parts for just about everything on board; and the crew was well versed in the basics of

Adele, a Little Harbor 50, cuts easily to windward on her way across the Atlantic—a well-designed boat, sailed by a competent skipper, making a classic passage.

boat handling, seamanship and maintenance. *Adele* was a self-sufficient, ocean-sailing boat, which is a tribute to her owner and skipper, who had taken the care to prepare himself, his boat and his crew for the task at hand.

Such is the formula for successful cruising.

OR THINGS CAN go dreadfully wrong.

Not everyone who sets out for a cruise—and it need not be across an ocean—takes the trouble to follow the lead of experienced off-shore sailors. The failure to do so, either because of inexperience or carelessness, can result in an unhappy ending, even disaster.

A dramatic example of a cruise gone bad was highly publicized during the summer of 1989—a disaster that became a cover story in the August 21, 1989, edition of *People* magazine, which is hardly the place you expect to find a sailing story. It is a paradigm of poor planning, poor preparation and poor seamanship. The tale was told to reporters by the survivor, Janet Culver. We will never know the other side of the story, because her friend and the skipper on the cruise, Nick Abbott, Jr., did not survive. His failure to bring the 37-foot sloop home safely ended in his own demise.

Janet Culver joined her boyfriend, Nick Abbott, in St. George's, Bermuda, in June, planning to sail with him on the 650-mile passage to Greenport, New York. It was the right time of the year for the trip, too early for a threat from hurricanes, too late for a serious northerly gale to hit them during the Gulf Stream crossing. The 37-foot sloop *Anaulis* had done some ocean sailing and was equipped with electronics and an autopilot, although the autopilot was not working. In fact, one of the reasons Nick had invited Janet to accompany him was the simple need aboard for another helmsperson. Janet didn't realize until several days later that the broken autopilot was symptomatic of the general condition of *Anaulis*.

The couple set off on a perfect day and at once started making miles for New York. But, not having a shortwave radio aboard and having failed to contact local meteorologists for a forecast, Nick was surprised the first night out to find they had sailed directly into a passing tropical depression. Three days of rough weather, rain, wind and lumpy seas followed, during which Janet suffered from seasickness that kept her in her berth while off watch. Nick began to suffer as well, although not from seasickness. He gradually became morose and dissatisfied with the condition of his crew. According to Janet, Nick became increasingly demeaning and critical of his partner on the cruise.

On the night of their fourth day out of Bermuda, they sailed into the back side of the passing depression and once again had strong winds and rain. Choosing to heave-to for the night, Nick tried to shorten sail. Yet his efforts were interrupted when he discovered a loose sheet tangled in the propeller. At this point, fearing the loss of the auxiliary, Nick panicked. In Janet's account, she says he knew he could only run the engine in neutral, yet somehow managed to start the auxiliary in gear. Quickly shutting the engine down, Nick tried to shift the transmission into neutral and once again started the engine. Somehow, he had left the engine in gear. The propeller bound on the sheet, the torque of the engine bent the shaft and as it did, the shaft tore a huge hole out of the boat where the stuffing box had been fiberglassed in place.

What had started as a routine problem, one that could have been sorted out when the weather calmed down, had turned into a survival situation.

Anaulis began to sink quickly. Nick and Janet had no choice but to abandon ship. Yet they had no life raft. Their only hope was their inflatable dinghy. Having failed to prepare an abandon-ship kit, Nick and Janet hurriedly gathered food and other items from around the boat and desperately tried to load it into the dinghy. They managed to bring along fishing gear, some food in the refrigerator and Nick's sextant. Yet, in their panicked exit from *Anaulis*, they only managed to bring with them half a gallon of fresh water and no canned food.

Within minutes, they were in the raft; they pushed off and watched the sinking hull drift away into the darkness. They were alone on the open sea, without the cover of a life raft, without much fresh water, without an emergency position-indicating radio beacon (EPIRB), without having sent a Mayday signal on the radio and without much hope of rescue. It was a desperate situation.

Without water and shelter, Janet's and Nick's health deteriorated rapidly. As they became weaker, they also began to lose their will to save themselves. On the ninth day, having become despondent, Nick Abbott stripped off his clothing, said goodbye to Janet and swam away. He did not get far before he sank exhausted beneath the waves. As Janet said later, Nick blamed himself for their predicament and could not reconcile himself to such a failure.

For four more days, Janet lay in the raft, gradually starving to death and withering under the heat of the summer sun. On the fourteenth day, just after a small fish had flopped into the dinghy, giving her an ounce of hope, Janet saw a sail passing a few hundred yards away. She desperately waved an orange life jacket, which, miraculously, the crew of the sailboat saw. An hour later, Janet was aboard the school vessel *Geronimo* in the capable hands of her skipper, Stephen Connett. Luck and endurance had brought her through.

Looking at the tale of the loss of *Anaulis*, the death of Nick Abbott and the miraculous rescue of Janet Culver, one has to conclude that the voyage was an accident waiting to happen. A list of everything Abbott and Culver did wrong would be long. It is fair to say, however, that *Anaulis* left Bermuda ill prepared for the 700-mile passage to New York. The trip was a delivery, so skipper Abbott was not prepared to buy expensive gear, such as a life raft, an EPIRB and a shortwave receiver, which most offshore sailors consider vital pieces of safety equipment. While the skipper was experienced, he set out with only one crew member, who was green and had little sailing experience. Seasickness, so often the bane of offshore sailing, took its toll by keeping Janet in her berth, thereby taxing Nick's strength and patience. No doubt the basic boat-handling mistake that led to the holing of *Anaulis*'s hull stemmed in large part from Nick's exhaustion.

By setting off without a forecast, Nick and Janet opened themselves up to needless hardship. The tropical depression they had to endure for three days would have been readily predicted and plotted by Bermuda meteorologists, by the high-seas broadcasts from Miami, New York or Portsmouth, Virginia. Failing to carry a shortwave receiver led directly to the ultimate disaster.

Lastly, the attitudes of both the skipper and the crew played important roles in the unhappy end to the story. We have only Janet's account upon which to base our hindsight, yet the facts of the story lead one to believe that she was unprepared for the rigors of a storm at sea and once she found herself in a storm withdrew to the point of being unable to contribute to the success of the passage. Nick, who had a lot of sailing experience, started the voyage casually and in good spirits. As the weather declined he became increasingly edgy, critical of his crew's behavior and erratic. Once in the dinghy, having lost *Anaulis*, he gradually lost hope and the will to survive. His deluded decision to swim away from the dinghy, away from Janet and his own failure as a skipper, must have seemed his only option.

In the two vastly different experiences—*Adele*'s transatlantic crossing and the loss of *Anaulis*—we have examples of the best and the worst of cruising under sail. The difference in the passages is not in the boats. Both were capable ocean sailing vessels. The difference lies in the different attitudes of the skippers and the methods they used to prepare for the tests of the sea.

The human factor is the most important ingredient in safe sailing. Taking the time to make considered and informed choices on how to get ready for a passage on the sea will most often lead to a pleasant and satisfying result. Keeping a cool head when bad weather and gear problems hit, as they occasionally will, leads to thoughtful decisions, workable contingency plans and, most often, a safe conclusion. Failing to prepare both boat and crew with care, taking lightly the awesome power of the sea can lead to disaster. Succumbing to exhaustion and panic, failing to have workable contingency plans and failing to carry the gear an emergency might require can lead to human errors that compound until a situation becomes dangerous.

The human factor: Our attitudes toward sailing and the sea make all the difference between safe sailing and unsafe sailing.

THE THREE Ps: PLANNING, PREPARATION AND PRACTICE

When you are beginning the process of getting yourself, your boat and your family and crew ready for coastal and offshore cruising, the Three Ps should be the cornerstones of that process. The Three Ps are: Planning, Preparation and Practice.

Seamanship, the art every sailor strives for and spends a lifetime perfecting, is largely made up of these three fundamentals. This book strives to illuminate the nature of seamanship as it applies to safety on the water. Most of the material deals with techniques and technical information. Yet the human factor, the most critical factor, includes attitudes, questions and points of view. The Three Ps are the keys to acquiring the point of view of an experienced seaman.

Planning

To lay useful and workable plans for coastal or offshore cruising, a sailor must know something about himself and about the type of sailing he will be doing. Will you sail at night and in the fog? Will you be forced by shoreside schedules to rush home on Sunday night no matter the weather? Will you cruise in cool seasons? Or in the tropics? By answering these questions and many more like them, you can paint a portrait of the type of planning you need to do. Most important in the planning process is defining the areas you'll be sailing in and the crew that will be on board.

What follows is a list of categories and questions that should be considered when planning to spend time on the open water:

Skipper's experience. What does he know and what does he need to learn more about?

Boat type. Does the boat require a large crew, or can it be sailed shorthanded? Does it require complex equipment, hence many spare parts? Can it beat to windward in strong breezes? Can it heave-to?

Sailing grounds. Will you be sailing close to home and close to safe harbors? Will you be sailing offshore? Will you be living aboard? Will it be cold or warm? Will the waters be deep or shallow, and how will that be affected by the depth of your keel?

Crew. Can the crew sail the boat without the skipper? Are crew members specialized in any aspect of sailing, such as navigation, engine maintenance, radio communications? Will there be crew aboard with special needs, such as children or older people?

Boat handling. Can sails be shortened quickly and easily? Does the crew know standard procedures, particularly the man-overboard drill? Does the boat carry appropriate anchor tackle that can be deployed quickly and easily?

Safety equipment. Does the boat carry required Coast Guard safety gear? Has safety gear been purchased and installed with thought given to its use in an emergency? Can each crew member deploy each item of safety gear? Has gear been upgraded to the highest standards?

The planning that goes into setting up a boat and its crew for sailing on open waters involves all of the above and much more. It would be impossible to list all the categories and questions a skipper should address when planning for safe sailing; the above list highlights the essentials.

Preparation

The preparation of a boat for open-water sailing, for longer coastal cruises and offshore passages, is the most important way of ensuring a safe sailing experience. Planning, as outlined above, will open a skipper's mind to the many tasks that lie ahead. But it is in the actual preparation of the boat that the seeds of a successful time on the water are sown. As we saw in the case of Nick Abbott and *Anaulis*, failure to complete even the most fundamental preparations can, on rare occasions, lead to disaster.

The preparation of a boat can take as long as you have time to spend on it, and it can cost as much as you have to spend. Ultimately, preparations are never done. It is important, then, to know at the outset that there will be limits, from both a time and a financial point of view. These limits have stirred many sailors to choose small cruising boats that can be made seaworthy with a minimum of time and a reasonably small amount of money. The idea is to go sailing, not to spend all summer, and all next summer, getting ready to go. Too often, the choice of a large boat with complex systems, heavy and complicated rigs and vast accommodations leads to a lengthy and frustrating period of preparation.

The trick is to draw a balance. A boat should be large enough to handle the types of seas you may face and should have accommodations for the crew. But a boat should not exceed an owner's ability to maintain it and pay for it. If it does, plans to go cruising will fade as enthusiasm is buried under endless projects.

With that in mind, what follows is a list of categories and questions on the basics of preparing a vessel for time on the water.

The skipper. Has he sailed enough to be competent in a variety of situations? Or, should he prepare himself by attending a sailing school or by sailing with others who have more experience? Is he well organized? Does he savor the responsibility of being skipper?

The hull. Is the hull sound? Is the hull-to-deck joint watertight? Are ports and hatches watertight? Do through-hulls have appropriate sea cocks that work? Are the rudder and steering systems sound and in good working order? Have adequate pumps been installed?

The deck. Is the deck laid out for safe sailing? Are sufficient handholds provided? Can safety harnesses be clipped on quickly and easily? Is the crew protected from spray, rain and wind? Are sheets and halyards led so sails can be handled efficiently and safely from the cockpit? Are stanchions through-hull mounted or installed with backing plates? Is deck hardware strong enough and well enough installed to function well in poor weather? Can gear carried on deck be lashed down? Are the anchors and rodes handy, yet well secured? Does the cockpit have scuppers large enough to drain the away a boarding wave?

The rig. Is the mast set up straight? Is the standing rigging strong enough to withstand the expected strains? Are the halyards led properly and of sufficient strength? Are the spreaders set up properly? Can the boom be controlled by a traveler, vang or preventer? Is the boom's gooseneck robust and in good repair? Is the mast stepped on deck? Is it stepped on the keel? Are the partners— where the mast passes through the deck—snug and watertight?

Down below. Are sufficient handholds provided? Can the galley be used when the boat is hard on the wind and heeled over? Are there sea berths set up so the crew can rest or sleep in warmth and dryness? Can the navigator work with charts and navigation equipment uninterrupted? Are essential stores, such as food, spare parts and dry clothing, well organized and easily accessible?

Engineering. Is an operating auxiliary engine essential to the running of the vessel? Has it and the battery-charging system been thoroughly serviced? Is battery capacity adequate to the current drains of lights, electronics and other systems, such as refrigeration? Are there backup systems for bilge pumps, freshwater pumps and cabin lighting? Are engine systems and the hatches covering them secured against a knockdown and possible inversion of the hull?

Electronics and navigation. Are basic electronics serviceable? Can the onboard systems provide basic information, such as depth, speed and miles logged, to navigate by dead reckoning in poor weather? Are mechanical backup systems available should electronics fail? Have the compasses been swung? Is the crew capable of both electronic navigation and traditional piloting? Is celestial navigation part of the navigation plan?

As in the discussion of planning for safe sailing, the above list does not cover every aspect of the preparations that must be considered prior to sailing any significant distance. However, the questions asked and the answers provided by those engaged in preparing a boat will add up to a well-founded vessel, a prepared and vigilant crew and an attitude aboard that is prepared to meet the challenges of the sea.

Practice

No aspect of seamanship and safe sailing is more often preached by the pundits and so seldom employed as the third of the Three Ps. With the best-laid plans in hand, with a well found and fitted out boat, most sailors set out to gain their experience on the job. The essential time spent practicing shipboard routines while close to home and in calm waters is all too often omitted from the sailing schedule.

This is understandable. Sailing and long-distance cruising usually must be undertaken in the few precious hours and days wedged between the more serious business of work and home life. Having just a few days or weeks to enjoy a boat and a vacation, most of us choose not to sacrifice a portion of that time practicing the routines and drills for which the boat and its systems have been prepared. The skipper, who often has the most experience and the least need for practice, should realize that a few hours spent practicing with the crew will accomplish several desirable things at once.

Practicing onboard routines will serve to inform crew members of the whereabouts of essential gear, so that gear can be found under stress and possibly in darkness. Practicing will bring to the fore omissions in planning and preparation that may have been overlooked or deemed nonessential. Practicing will help the whole crew to understand the skipper's standards of safety and seamanship. And, importantly, practicing will bind a crew together at the outset of a time spent on the water instead of during the trip or after.

The aspects of sailing that should be practiced with all the crew on board will obviously be those pertaining to emergencies. Yet there are other routines, such as sail handling, meal preparation, radio communications and navigation that should also be included on the list of items to practice prior to setting out for parts unknown.

Below is a list of categories and questions that may be useful when thinking about what should be practiced with the crew and how to go about spending practice time.

Sail handling. Do all crew members know how sheets and halyards are led? Who can tie in reefs and shorten sail? How will the foredeck be covered? Are storm sails aboard and easily accessible? Does the crew know how to set storm canvas? What is the sail-shortening sequence? How will the boat be rigged when hove-to?

Man overboard. Is the man-overboard gear accessible and easily deployed? Does each crew member know his or her job during a man-overboard emergency? Who will be in charge should the skipper be in the water? Is the pick-up maneuver clear to everyone? Can an injured crew be hoisted aboard quickly?

Fire. Are flammable fuels stored below decks? Does the crew know where fire extinguishers and other fire-fighting gear is stored? Does everyone aboard know how to use the equipment? How will crew below exit the cabin in an emergency?

Collisions. Does the crew know the rules of the road? Can each crew member anticipate a collision in time to make a course correction? Is the crew familiar with the running lights of commercial vessels?

Water in the boat. Do all crew members know the location of sea cocks and pumps? Does each crew member know his or her job if flooding becomes an emergency? Are pumps on board adequate to handle rapid flooding? Can the engine be used to discharge water? Have provisions been made to repair a broken through-hull or patch a hole in the hull?

Abandon ship. Is a life raft and an abandon-ship kit accessible and easily deployed? Has survival in a raft or in a dinghy been planned for and adequately prepared for? Does everyone know how to deploy survival gear? Have radio procedures been established?

Practicing the routines for dealing with emergencies can be a sobering experience for all on board, if only because it forces the crew to contemplate the worst that can happen while sailing. Practicing should be serious business. But to make those hours of practice truly worthwhile, it is important that the skipper and crew work to make the routines both fun and engaging. Should an emergency arise, teamwork, an attitude of competence and cool-headedness will serve the crew well, while confusion and panic will only compound a deteriorating situation.

The Three Ps provide a foundation for seamanship. Out on the open water, the pleasures of sailing unfettered by shoreside constraints depend in large part on the thoroughness of the planning, the attention to details during preparations and the practiced competence of those sailing together.

THE SELF-RELIANT SKIPPER

In June 1985, a young woman aged 18 sailed her 26-foot sloop *Varuna* into St. George's, Bermuda. She was alone and had just completed a harrowing but successful trip from New York. It was to be the first leg of a cruise that would take her around the world over the next two and a half years.

Tania Aebi, whose story has been widely read in the pages of *Cruising World* magazine and in her book, *Maiden Voyage*, set out as wet behind the ears as any novice skipper. She had sailed some

Although only 18 when she departed New York on her solo trip around the world, Tania Aebi quickly learned the satisfactions of being a self-reliant sailor.

6,000 miles offshore with her father on a voyage from England to the Caribbean and then home to New York. But the trip to Bermuda was her first in command and her first sailing solo.

Something happened to Tania during that first leg of her circumnavigation. She evolved from a knee-knocking girl into a competent offshore skipper. She likes to tell the story of her first day in Bermuda. After rushing ashore to call home to let family and friends know that she had arrived safely, she found herself in a quayside restaurant and bar frequented by the transient sailors in St. George's. She was still just the eighteen-year-old who had left New York. She still looked even younger than her age. But the men at the bar, who had all sailed in from distant ports, didn't see her that way. They spoke to her as an adult. They listened to her as an adult. She wasn't, in their eyes, a dewy-eyed kid; she was one of them.

Tania's first offshore passage was no model of seamanship. But she had mastered her boat, had puzzled through her navigation and had made a safe landfall after 700 miles. She had new good reasons to trust her own judgment and competence. She had become self-reliant, and the others in the bar that day in Bermuda knew it. And she knew it.

MOST SAILORS DON'T head off to sea alone, nor do they tackle such ambitious adventures as Tania's. Yet every sailor who skippers his or her own vessel should strive to become self-reliant. Self-reliance should be an attitude as well as a fact. Sailing with a skipper who doesn't have confidence in himself or in his ship is a torturous experience and a fundamentally unsafe one. If doubt and indecision rule, then neither the skipper nor the crew will be able to enjoy their time on the water. Without clear standards of seamanship and an orderly sailing routine, small incidents can quickly become emergencies and emergencies can develop into unmanageable disasters.

Experience is the best teacher of self-reliance. No book can hope to instill confidence and competence by providing instruction and passing along experience secondhand. But for those who will be skippering their own vessels, there are some attitudes that may prove useful and some models of seamanship it may be wise to emulate.

Miles and Beryl Smeeton, who sailed their 42-foot ketch *Tzu Hang* all over the world in the 1950s and '60s, were often asked why they chose not to carry a shortwave transceiver aboard. They sailed to the far corners of the globe, south to Cape Horn and north to the Aleutian Islands. Miles said that he and his wife and their daughter had chosen to seek out a life at sea and to sail far from the beaten track; they carried no radio because they did not wish to rely on the goodness of others to bail them out of a situation of their own making. And they did not wish others to risk and possibly lose their lives attempting to rescue amateur sailors who had gone to sea for pleasure.

In our day and age, sailing without radio equipment is a more extreme action to take than it was twenty years ago. The world is buzzing with means of communication that can prove extremely useful to sailors. Single sideband transceivers and emergency position-indicating radio beacons (EPIRBs) have their place on any oceangoing vessel. The question is not whether to carry radios, but when and how to use them. The choice depends upon a skipper's sense of self-reliance.

The fundamental attitude shared by most veteran seaman is that if you call for help—a Mayday—then you must abandon your fate to your rescuers, if and when they arrive. This is the starting point for developing the whole range of attitudes that mark the experienced skipper, the man or woman with sea time and the right, resolute sense of responsibility.

In 1980, Lloyd Bergeson found himself on the threshold of a decision that would mark him as an amateur or a seaman. He had sailed his classic New York 30 across the Atlantic from Massachusetts to his family homeland in Norway the summer before. The trip, long dreamed of and planned for, had been successful. His boat, *Cockatoo II*, had acquitted herself well, the transatlantic passage went off without a hitch and the summer season of cruising Norway had been wonderful.

What remained, in that next summer, was the return trip home to the United States.

Bergeson was an experienced skipper. A member of the Cruising Club of America, he had sailed in numerous offshore races and had cruised extensively along the East Coast from New York to Nova Scotia. He had learned seamanship in the old school and was meticulous about boat care, boat handling and on-the-water vigilance. He epitomized the qualities of the Three Ps.

It was with a great deal of distress, then, that several days out from England on his way home—taking the northern route across the Atlantic—Bergeson discovered that *Cockatoo II* was leaking badly. The old wood one-design that had been his companion over many summer seasons of cruising and racing was breaking down under the strain of high-latitude sailing. The vessel that had carried Bergeson to the homeland of his father and grandfather was going to sink.

Bergeson did what every experienced skipper would do. He bore away from the wind to ease the strain on the old hull. He studied the problem and sought a way to stop the leaks. He pumped, and his son, his only crew, pumped. Convinced that he would be putting his son's life and his own in jeopardy by sailing unassisted back to

England, Bergeson took what was for him a drastic step. He switched on his EPIRB.

Close to the North Atlantic shipping lanes and under the flight paths of the New York–to–Heathrow air traffic, the EPIRB's bleat was picked up quickly, and within a matter of hours a ship had found *Cockatoo II* and hove-to to windward of her. Bergeson knew what he had to do. But he had doubts, as any man would. Running downwind toward England, the old boat had settled down, and the leak was not completely unmanageable, which meant Bergeson and his son were still pumping thirty minutes of every hour. They possibly could make it on their own to a safe harbor. Or possibly not.

Bergeson's decision to abandon *Cockatoo II* and accept the assistance of the ship was one of the hardest of his life. Despite a glimmer of hope that he might be able to save his much-loved boat, he knew that setting off his EPIRB was an irrevocable act. He had called Mayday. It is the ultimate call. Once answered, he knew he could not refuse the help tendered to him. To do so would not only be an insult to the ship's captain, it would violate the traditional trust of sailors assisting one another on the high seas.

Broken and sinking, *Cockatoo II* was left to end her days under the waves of the North Atlantic. In the story of her demise and of the last hours aboard her, Lloyd Bergeson provided those who read his stories and those who know him with a stern lesson about what self-reliance on the high seas can and should mean.

At sea, your life is in your own hands. Should you ever have to use the worldwide network—SarSat, Cospas or Amver—you sign off as the master of your own ship and place your fate in the hands of your rescuers. Losing a wonderful boat is a terrible sacrifice. For a proud and capable seaman, losing one's own self-reliance can be an even worse blow.

THE SELF-RELIANT SKIPPER rarely faces the ultimate decision of whether or not to call for help with a Mayday or EPIRB call. More often, as skipper of your own boat you will be faced with breakages that can dampen a passage and, if ignored, possibly end it. Attrition of gear and of shipboard systems may be the single greatest hazard confronting those who set off to fend for themselves on the sea.

The problem of breakages is not solely the province of offshore sailors. Modern cruising boats are complex machines, requiring a master who can not only wield parallel rules and a sailmaker's palm, but must also have an idea of how electrical systems work, what makes a diesel stop and go, and how a diaphragm pump looks when disassembled and, importantly, what it should look like when reassembled.

Coastal sailor or bluewater man, the modern self-reliant skipper must be a handy fellow. Unless you are prepared to stop at every available boatyard with your credit card pinned to your breast pocket, it is important to adopt the attitude that if you can't fix it, you must be able to carry on without it. That simple statement carries a vast amount of responsibility with it.

In the winter of 1986–87, Richard McBride faced a breakdown that could, if things were not set right, have led to a very serious survival situation. McBride, a New Zealander, had sailed in the first BOC Challenge Singlehanded Around-the-World Race. He had finished, which was a victory in itself, and had overcome being stranded on the Falkland Islands after rounding Cape Horn. But in the winter of 1986 he was on another mission, a delivery trip from Newport, Rhode Island, to New Zealand via Panama, as skipper of the 50-foot Whitbread boat *Outward Bound*.

The boat was a high-powered offshore racing machine that had won its class in the 1985–86 Whitbread Around-the-World Race. She had been built and driven by New Zealander Digby Taylor, but McBride was to be her skipper for the 12,000-mile journey home. All went well for the first leg of the trip, from Newport to Panama, but on the second leg, across the South Pacific, something went wrong. In a black squall that rode down on them in the trade winds, *Outward Bound*'s tired rigging gave way and the mast came down.

Two thousand miles from home, McBride had two choices. He could press a button and summon help from the worldwide search-and-rescue network, or he could patch things up and sail on. Knowing that search-and-rescue coverage in the South Pacific is spotty at best, and being handy with his tools, McBride did not have to consider long which course he would take. He and his crew would build a jury-rigged spar and sail home under their own power.

When *Outward Bound* had been fitted out for the Whitbread race, Digby Taylor had brought aboard spares to meet virtually any contingency the race might offer. McBride now put those spares to good use. Simple items, such as bulldog clamps, a pop-riveting gun, spare halyards, turnbuckles and shrouds, a sailmaker's kit and a full tool kit, enabled the crew to scavenge the broken spar and rig a stable replacement. It took McBride and his crew three days— days spent drifting and rolling miserably in the trade winds—to rerig *Outward Bound*. But when the job was done, it had been done well.

When they set their cut-down sails and started *Outward Bound* sailing again, they had 2,000 miles of sailing ahead of them. The progress they made, under jury rig, would be the envy of any cruising boat. Some 15 days later, having averaged better than six knots for the passage, *Outward Bound* sailed into Auckland. As the local fleet of boats came out to meet her—the Whitbread class winner and the disabled passagemaker—all were astounded to find her screaming up Hauraki Gulf at eight knots. Her crew was rested and well. Despite her truncated rig, she looked shipshape. What could have been an ignominious return was instead a triumph.

The right spare parts aboard, a full tool kit, able hands, a willingness to tackle a problem and solve it in a seamanlike way—planning, preparation and practice—that is what the return of *Outward Bound* was all about. Her skipper knew what he had to do to make a success of a broken passage, and he did it. He was self-reliant.

SELF-RELIANCE IS A goal of many skippers. It is the mark of those with sea time and those with a gift for the sea. To sail safely, no matter where the course is set, the master of the vessel has to be the master of the situation. The following list may help you to remember the lessons taught by the experiences related in this section:

- To arrive safely and to lead those who sail with you, you need to trust your instincts, trust your navigation and trust those who sail with you.
- You don't have to know everything before you set sail. You do have to be willing to learn everything.

- Small problems aboard must be dealt with quickly, otherwise they soon become large problems, and large problems rapidly become disasters.
- We sail for pleasure and adventure, so we have no automatic right to be saved from our own mistakes.
- A call for help—a Mayday or EPIRB alert—must be real, for it is irrevocable.
- A Mayday or EPIRB alert informs all who hear it that you are eagerly prepared to abandon your own boat in favor of the rescuers'.
- You have to be handy enough and well-prepared enough to repair broken gear, or you must be prepared to carry on without it.
- The gear on board vital to your survival must be the gear you can mend yourself.

A COUPLE IS A TEAM

A majority of those who set out sailing do so as couples or families. Often, the push to take up sailing and cruising comes from the man in the group, while the woman finds herself involved without having the experience to know in advance what she will enjoy most about sailing. No doubt the traditional role of skipper—which many men embrace with gusto—tends to relegate the women in the party to secondary and therefore uninteresting roles aboard the boat.

When you hear a skipper at the wheel of his new production 36-footer bellowing at his wife at the bow while she's doing her level best to heave the 45-pound plow over the lifelines, you don't have to wonder why she might prefer simple pursuits like skydiving or fire walking to sailing. The wonder is that so many couples do in fact make successful partners aboard ship.

For most cruising people, the ability to work as a team marks the difference between safe sailing and unsafe sailing. If there is only one person aboard who can navigate or who knows how to use the radios or who can reef in high winds, then the other member of the crew is forever at the mercy of the keeper of skills and knowledge.

Miles and Beryl Smeeton, an English couple who ventured far and wide aboard their 44-foot ketch *Tzu Hang* in the 1950s and '60s, were an excellent example of a couple working together on an equal footing and sailing always as a team.

Should he take an untimely swim, he'll soon know the folly of his pride.

The sailing life offers a unique environment for men and women to work together as a team. Aboard a boat, even if only for a weekend, the well-being of all aboard depends upon cooperation, planning, forethought, the execution of sometimes complex maneuvers—all the qualities one might find in a fine doubles partnership in tennis or bridge. And it is a mistake to think that conforming to the traditional roles of men and women is always the best way to proceed.

Miles and Beryl Smeeton again come to mind. They were a dynamic pair who took to sailing in their forties after they felt they had become too old to continue mountain climbing at the level they had become accustomed to—above 18,000 feet. The sea offered another challenge, one they could face together. As they played it, Beryl was the spark that ignited their plans. It was her vision that drew the couple to the Horn, not once but three times. She led them on an east-about circumnavigation, against the wind and currents. It was Beryl who took great pleasure in planning journeys that would take *Tzu Hang* where no cruising boat had gone before.

Miles, a towering man of six feet, six inches, was not simply a follower. He was a retired brigadier general in the British army. He had been much decorated in the Second World War. He stood tall among men. But in the team he formed with Beryl, he more often than not found himself being the implementor of her grand dreams instead of the sole active partner. Miles navigated and ran the ship. He lorded it over maintenance and seamanship. He made the dreams real.

Together they made a classic and marvelous pair.

But most couples who take to sailing together don't naturally fall into such a pattern. Instead, they have to learn the ropes of how to work together as shipmates. They have to find ways to live in the confines of a boat, to make decisions and to carry out plans as a team.

There are a few places around the world favored by cruising boats on long passages. Such passages can be hell for couples that have not become a team. In Gibraltar or Barbados or Panama or Tahiti, it is not uncommon to witness a cruising boat make up to a quay and to see the female member of the crew waiting on deck with her bags packed, only to leap off the boat as soon as it comes close enough to the quay. Something has gone wrong, and the only solution is an airplane home.

One of the most common reasons for a mutiny is the failure of the skipper to share the whole voyage with his teammate. A good example of how this happens and how it can be overcome occurred during a three-year cruise undertaken by Jim and Nina Hunt aboard the O'Day 40 *Whale and the Bird.* Jim has been a sailor all his life, had been in the sailing business for twenty-five years and knew his way around a cruising boat as well as any man. In his last working position before setting off he had been president of the O'Day Corporation and was thus responsible for building more sailing boats than just about any man alive. When his time came to take a few years off, he was ready.

Nina was ready, too. Sort of. She was not an old salt. She sailed and had cruised with Jim for years. But sailing was his thing, cruising was his passion, and offshore passage making was not something high on her list. As *Whale and the Bird* cruised south from the East Coast to the Caribbean, wintered in the islands and then headed off for a season in the Mediterranean, Jim often brought crew along for the offshore runs. These were guys who were happy to get offshore, who relished the challenge and who shared a manly spirit of teamwork aboard the boat.

Nina, in those days, often preferred to fly. She knew, as many sailing wives know, that nothing goes to windward like a 747. Why fight it when you can hop over it?

But after sailing together for months in the Med, after sailing together, with crew, back across the Atlantic and after another winter in the islands, Nina had become a convert. Over those months, she had gone from being a passenger aboard her own boat to being the other member of a two-person team. She took over radio duty and handled all communication chores. She took over the chart table and handily piloted *Whale and the Bird* hither and thither. Nina and Jim gradually began to divide work more evenly and the satisfaction they both derived from the division aided the success of their cruise.

They had never sailed offshore alone together. But when they were in Bermuda on their way home to Massachusetts in the spring of 1989, they could find no crew to help them. They could leave the boat until a crew could join them. Or they could sail her home together. Jim says it was Nina's idea. She doesn't disagree. They set off, just the two of them, and had a marvelous passage home across the Gulf Stream, sailing for five days, watch on and watch off, each always relying on the other to hold up his or her end. They both agree it was the best passage of the whole voyage.

They arrived back where they had started, having seen some of the world and having removed themselves from the treadmill for a time. They were the same couple. But they were changed. They had become a team.

There are thousands of similar stories that vary in detail but remain constant in overall theme. In the end, the success of a couple's cruising experience and the safety of the boat and its crew depends upon teamwork.

To summarize, here are a few dos and don'ts to help couples work toward teamwork:

- Begin as equals. If one member of the couple is not an adept sailor, send him or her to sailing school. The success of some endeavors, like learning to drive or learning to sail, may be best left to professionals.
- Preparation and stocking of the boat should be a joint effort. If you don't know where the soup is stored, how can you cook dinner?
- The deck layout and deck systems should be worked out so one person can work the sails, handle the anchor gear and otherwise tend ship while the other steers or sleeps. All of these systems should be worked out in such a way that brute strength is not the first requirement for use.
- Deck work should be shared. No one likes tying down a loose sail when the wind is up and the rain is pelting down. Why should one person have to do it every time?
- Don't hog the helm. Or, conversely, don't always avoid the helm. Steering can be exciting, and it can be dull. No one should end up with only one or the other.
- Do maintenance together as much as possible. Hands-on experience during routine onboard chores, whether changing en-

gine oil or changing the sheets, will keep all informed on where
things are kept, how they work and what condition the gear is in.
- Practice as a team, switching responsibilities from time to time.
  If one or the other suddenly needs to handle the boat alone,
  such practice will be a great help.
- Listen while the other person talks. This is the most difficult
  onboard task. However, those who have mastered it report that
  it creates miraculous results.

SETTING SAFE GOALS FOR A SAFE CRUISE

When you take to the sea, you put yourself at the mercy of wind and
wave and tide. These are things over which you have no control, so it
only makes sense to lay plans that are flexible enough to bend under
a fickle wind change, a mean streak of weather or a foul current.
Most often you will arrive where you intend to. Yet, it is surprising
how often, if you spend enough time sailing and cruising, you will
find yourself someplace else altogether. Should you be forced to
alter course and alter your destination, safety dictates that you be
prepared to navigate in areas off your original course.

A contingency plan for every leg of a cruise is essential to the
setting of a safe cruising plan. Carry the charts and guides you will
need, not only for the areas along that thick pencil line you've drawn
on the chart, but also for the coasts and harbors along the way.
Equipping yourself with extra charts involves an additional expense. But the expense will seem small should you be forced to
enter a strange harbor under the duress of wind and weather.

Setting safe goals for a cruise begins with such contingency planning. Just as important, it is vital for the skipper and the crew to
appreciate the capabilities of the boat, the abilities of the crew and
the types of conditions that can be expected ahead.

Most sailors fit their sailing and cruising into the narrow cracks of
time between work, family commitments and the running of a
household. They leap up from their desks on a Friday afternoon,
heads filled with the details of busy lives, and step aboard their
boats with grand plans to sail off for a few days or a few weeks. No

matter how experienced the crew, it will take a day or two for all aboard to get their sea legs, overcome seasickness and fall into the rhythm of the sea. A prudent skipper will plan for such a break-in period and will set courses accordingly.

The first day or two of a cruise should involve short runs and practice time for the crew in protected waters. It takes time to refamiliarize yourself and your crew with sheet-lead placements, with reefing systems, with the workings of the Loran, depth sounder and other complex electronic aids. Time spent going over all the systems and sharing the skills of how to manage them with the rest of the crew is time well spent. Such a beginning can lead to famous runs later, when everyone and everything aboard is ship shape.

Scheduling is often the single most important factor in planning a cruise. A schedule, like the choice of sleeping apparel, is a very personal thing. Some sailors progress along an intended course with the speed of a snail, stopping at every available harbor, sampling every beach, every shop and restaurant. Others have distant destinations in mind and rush headlong toward them, damning the head winds, the torpedoes and just about anything else in their way. Most of us fall somewhere in between.

The trick with scheduling, whether you are a snail or a hare, is to leave enough slack, enough flexibility in the schedule to allow for the unforeseen. If you plan to meet friends at a distant anchorage, you will do well to leave yourself an extra day along the way. You may not need it. Or you may. Engines break down. Anchors get snagged. Thunder squalls and strong head winds can cross your path. Leaving an extra day in the plan will allow you the luxury of not going out when you don't want to or don't have to or can't.

Too many accidents have marred a sailing experience because the crew was pressing on when tired, when sick or in bad weather, simply because there was an important appointment at the other end of the cruise. No one ever lost a friend or a job or a business because he was delayed by bad weather. No one ever suffered because she had an extra day built into her schedule. A day off, even a day off from cruising, can be welcome.

Setting safe goals for a safe cruise requires the skipper and crew to be honest about what they can and can't do, what they will and won't do, and why they have chosen to take to sailing together. To summarize the points discussed:

- Always have a contingency plan, as well as needed charts and guides, should you be forced to change your destination in midstream.
- Maintain a flexible attitude about achieving destinations. If you don't make it to that far harbor this year, there's always next year.
- Plan a break-in period at the beginning of a cruise for both the skipper and the crew. Let everyone get their sea legs before asking them to really go to sea.
- Leave slack in a sailing schedule, a day here and there for downtime, for maintenance or to meet the needs of some change in plans. Rushing can cause mistakes and accidents.
- Choose your weather. No matter what the schedule says, it is vital to make sailing decisions based upon present conditions and not upon airline reservations, business appointments or an invitation to cocktails.

THE HUMAN FACTOR is the most important element when going to sea. You may have the best boat, and the top gear and have taken every sailing course offered. But if you have not adopted a seamanlike attitude toward your boat, your crew and your sailing, none of it will make a difference.

Experience is a great teacher. The safety-minded skipper will gather his experience slowly and deliberately and will always keep a weather eye on those who sail with him.

Chapter 2

CHOOSING A SAFE BOAT

Designed for Safety
Constructed for Safety
Five Rules for Choosing a Safe Boat

THE CHOICE OF a boat in which to sail and cruise depends on a number of factors. Our boats are in many ways emblems of ourselves. They reflect our sense of taste, our affluence, our experience and, most importantly, our plans for where and how we will sail.

It would be impossible to put down on paper much that would be helpful on the aesthetics of sailboats. No matter how long a person has been involved with boats and sailing, he is sure to have formed a clear idea of what looks sweet in a boat and what doesn't. The old adage among yacht brokers and dealers advises those in the market for a new boat to only buy a boat they fall in love with. That's sound advice, although there is no telling why one person will think a particular boat is a beauty while the next fellow will scoff at it.

The matter of affluence is even harder to nail. Some sailors, no matter the size of their bank balance, choose to sail in small pocket cruising boats, in trailer sailers or compact keel boats. Yet next to

The Navy 44 was designed to replace the venerable Luders 44s that have served the U.S. Naval Academy Sailing Team for the last quarter of a century. The boats were conceived to be fast, able ocean-sailing vessels and incorporate the best in performance, comfort and safety features.

them in the anchorage you will find another sailor, of modest means, who has sacrificed much to sail in a boat that stretches his ability to pay for it. One takes pride in his ability to enjoy sailing without suffering the slings and arrows of financial worry, the other takes pride in his ability to handle and maintain the ultimate object of his seafaring dreams.

Sailing should be fun, and owning a boat is a large part of that fun. In choosing a boat that suits you and your family, you should place the notion of fun high on the list. That is why so many pundits advise those looking for new boats to buy a boat that does not strain the checkbook and therefore does not strain the home financial front. If the new boat is a drain on the checkbook, requiring many other sacrifices, then chances are good that those who are supposed to enjoy this object of beauty will come to resent it. It has happened before. It will happen again.

However, choosing a tiny cruiser can also have a downside. If the checkbook looks great but the new boat can't comfortably house the sailing crew for a wet weekend, then the boat won't get the use originally planned for it.

It's always a compromise.

One assumption those in the market for a new cruising boat often mistakenly make is that the larger you go, the safer you will be. Size will affect both speed and seakeeping abilities, both of which are safety factors. But there are many small cruising boats that have sailed long and competent voyages while their larger counterparts remained securely moored in the marina. If the small cruiser is well found and fitted out, and if it is sailed competently, it can offer its crew the world, although it will be a world without hot showers, ice cream and a large library.

When young Tania Aebi and her father, Ernst, went looking for a boat for her to take around the world on her solo circumnavigation, they sought a vessel that would look after Tania. The boat had to have a hull that was robust, would handle the sea easily, would be kind to the crew by self-steering and would ride out a gale hove-to, if need be. Sails had to be of a size that could be managed by a 95-pound, 18-year-old girl. The anchor tackle had to be light enough to be retrieved without the aid of a windlass. The boat had to have an inboard diesel, but also had to sail well enough to get Tania off a lee shore, or through a coral pass.

After inspecting dozens of boats, Ernst and Tania finally chose a boat that had a long, distinguished pedigree. The boat was a Contessa 26, built by J. J. Taylor in Canada. The design was based on Scandinavian Folkboats, which had long proved to be able and seakindly. The fiberglass hull had a full keel, with the lead enclosed in the fiberglass. The large rudder was hung on the trailing edge of the keel and on the little boat's transom. Such a rudder is well protected when the boat is aground and is particularly good for affixing a self-steering gear. The rig was a simple, single-spreader masthead configuration, with sails small enough for Tania to handle them in just about any conditions.

The accommodations below were originally designed for a couple. For Tania, the space was ample for solo sailing. With fairly deep bilges and full ends forward and aft, there was plenty of storage room for the gear and supplies an offshore cruiser needed. And,

Tania Aebi's Contessa 26 *Varuna* was small for a round-the-world passage-maker, but the size and ease of handling made the boat perfect for Tania's needs. The success of her voyage is in large part due to the choice of the right boat for the job.

just as important, there was enough space aboard for Tania to stow away the treasures she collected as she visited islands and countries around the world.

Varuna, as Tania named her Contessa 26, was the perfect pocket cruising boat for the voyage around the world. But for most sailors a 26-footer would be the bare minimum. Moreover, for most, a boat of that size would not offer the speed and the comfort to make off-shore sailing a pleasure.

At the other extreme is Steve and Linda Dashew's new cruising boat, *Sundeer.* Designed by the Dashews as their own ultimate off-shore cruising boat, *Sundeer* follows in the wake of a decade of designing and building the Deerfoot line of boats. The Dashews' premise is to go long, lean and fast. Their Deerfoot boats are all over 60 feet, are of light displacement and shallow draft and carry very short rigs. Yet, because the boats are narrow on the waterline and have fair canoe-shaped hulls, the boats slide very easily through the water. *Sundeer,* at 67 feet, can be handled easily by two and will comfortably average 200 miles a day at sea. A complex boat that would strain many sailors' pocket books and exhaust their knowledge of onboard systems, for the Dashews *Sundeer* is the culmination of their 170,000 miles of offshore sailing, of their boat-building experience and of their own sailing preferences.

Somewhere in between *Varuna* and *Sundeer* most sailors will find the cruising boat that suits their wants, their needs and their financial and maintenance abilities. To make the right choice, it is important, first, to find a boat that you fall for like a ton of bricks; the boat should be a vision of beauty and function.

But once you've found a boat—or several—that fill the first requirement, it is equally important to stand back and judge the boat as dispassionately as possible. To do so, you need to evaluate the overall design of the boat, its construction and its detailing. A sailor looking for the right boat, the safe boat, must be somewhat schizophrenic: He must be a cold-hearted surveyor with a real twinkle in his eye.

DESIGNED FOR SAFETY

The world of yacht design has gone through a major upheaval in the decade of the 1980s. Following the disastrous Fastnet race of 1979, so well documented and analyzed by John Rousmaniere in his book *Fastnet Force 10,* many leading designers and sailors began to question the direction of design trends.

During that race, a Force 10 gale (48 to 55 knots) hit the fleet of 303 boats that was racing from southern England around Fastnet Rock off the southern tip of Ireland. In surveys taken by race organizers and in interviews conducted by Rousmaniere in preparation for writing his book, some very disturbing statistics came to light.

It is estimated that at least 18 boats were rolled a full 360 degrees. Twenty-four boats were abandoned, 5 sank and approximately 170 were rolled over until their masts hit the water. Also, it was reported that five boats became inverted—turned turtle—and remained upside down for periods between 30 seconds and five minutes. Lastly, and tragically, 15 sailors lost their lives to drowning or hypothermia.

The Cruising Club of America, which was preparing to run its biennial Newport-Bermuda race in the spring of 1980, took a hard look at the Fastnet race and began to study what could be done to prevent such a disaster from reoccurring.

The CCA's Technical Committee joined forces with the Technical Committee of the Measurement Handicap System (MHS) to see what caused the Fastnet disaster. Several experts in the field of yacht design and marine engineering became central players in a study that was to last for five years. Karl Kirkman, chairman of the Sailboat Committee of the Society of Naval Architects and Marine Engineers, yacht designer Olin Stephens, Richard McCurdy, chairman of the Safety at Sea Committee of the United States Yacht Racing Union, and Dan Strohmeier, who was a former president of SNAME, all undertook the various tasks of analyzing design attributes, weather attributes and safety preparations. The primary focus of the study was to determine how and why so many boats capsized.

In 1985 a final report was issued by USYRU and SNAME's Joint Committee on Safety from Capsizing. The 66-page document, which is available from the United States Yacht Racing Union (P.O. Box 209, Newport, Rhode Island 02840), details the research undertaken by the joint committee and offers several broad conclusions that help illuminate what is safe and what is not in hull and yacht design. While the focus of the work was to assess the capabilities—the likelihood of capsize—of boats designed under the various racing rules (International Offshore Rule, International Measurement System and the old CCA rule), the conclusions should affect the way all sailors think about design.

The conclusions of the report, in brief, are:

- Larger boats are less prone to capsize than smaller boats.
- A dismasted sailboat is more likely to capsize than a boat carrying her full rig.
- A boat has an inherent stability range, i.e., an angle of heel past which it will capsize. That stability range can be calculated from the boat's lines and specifications.
- Some modern boats, which have been designed to the IOR, or are designed to be particularly beamy, may remain inverted following a capsize. Boats with a stability range under 120 degrees may remain inverted for as long as two minutes.
- Boats lying sideways to a sea, particularly light, beamy vessels, are more likely to capsize than boats that are held bow to the sea or stern to the sea. It follows, then, that boats that are sailed actively in gale conditions and breaking seas are more likely to avoid capsize than those left to lie untended, beam to the sea.

The issue of whether or not a boat will capsize, and when and how it might suffer such a fate, is a key point for any sailor contemplating safe extended coastal or offshore cruising. By analyzing a boat's stability range, you can get a very good reading on how the boat will handle a gale at sea and how best to plan your own gale tactics. The Joint Committee sought a simple way for boat owners to arrive at a usable measurement of their boat's stability range.

The best approach is to have your boat—or prospective boat—measured by an IMS measurer. From the measurements, the USYRU measurement team can then calculate the boat's stability range. The USYRU has a record of the many production boats already measured, so it may be possible to purchase the IMS information, containing the stability information, from the Union.

Another approach is to use the simple Capsize Screening Formula, derived by the committee for use by average sailors who do not have access to IMS measurements and do not own a boat already on the USYRU's list. The formula, which assumes that the vessel in question is of a fairly standard type and of a size suitable for offshore sailing, gives a general guide to a boat's stability. The number played out by the formula is the result of comparing the boat's beam with its displacement, for excessive beam has been shown to contribute to a lack of ultimate stability, while displacement can be a determining factor in improving stability. The formula is as follows:

$$\text{Capsize Screening Number} = \sqrt[3]{\frac{\text{Boat's Maximum Beam} \div}{(\text{Gross Displacement} \div 64)}}$$

In English: Take the boat's gross displacement (in pounds), divide it by 64 and then take the cube root of the quotient. Now, take that cube root and divide it into the boat's maximum beam (in feet). The resulting capsize screening number should be two or less. In general, if the number is over two, the boat fails the screen. If the number is under two, the boat passes.

Using the Capsize Screening Formula, you will be able to get a quick idea of a boat's stability. However, you will want to explore the boat's full capsize characteristics before you decide to purchase it and set off sailing in open waters.

ASSESSING A BOAT'S stability range will give you a good idea of how the boat will behave in the worst conditions. But when looking at a boat's design with safety in mind, it is essential to evaluate the hull design both in general and specifically.

The trend to light, fast hulls that has dominated cruising and racing boats since the late 1960s has provided sailors with boats that offer a high level of performance and ample accommodations. The evolution of hull design from full keels with keel-hung rudders has been a function of building materials and engineering as much as it has been due to innovation on the part of designers. In the 1880s Nathanael Herreshoff, the Wizard of Bristol, developed what may be the first small sailing vessel with a fin keel and spade rudder. He discovered that the performance of such a hull configuration outperformed every other design option of the time. Yet the split keel and rudder did not find its way into wide use until the advent of fiberglass materials and the engineering made possible by the material.

Traditional boats of today, boats with full keels, keel-hung rudders and their propellers in an aperture, are descendants of working craft from a hundred years ago. The design is noted for its

seakindliness, its ability to carry heavy loads, and its slow and delib-
erate motion through the water. The design type evolved at a time
when all boats were built of wood. The simple engineering requirements of constructing a seaworthy sailing vessel in wood led designers and builders to craft the full-keel designs we know today. In
fact, the reason Nathanael Herreshoff's early fin-keeler did not lead
to similar designs in larger, oceangoing vessels was simply that the
materials required to make such a vessel strong, seaworthy and safe
did not exist at the time.

Yet small-boat design quickly followed Herreshoff's lead. The
Star boat, the 110 and 210 and other one-designs have long, distinguished histories. All three are fin-keelers with spade rudders. But
it was not until the 1960s that larger boats, ocean-sailing boats,
could be engineered safely using the split design type. William
Lapworth's Cal 40, designed in the early 1960s, led the way by
acquitting itself as a very fast sailing boat around the buoys, a
winner of offshore races and, importantly, a safe and seakindly
vessel. The design of the Cal 40 was made possible by the extra-

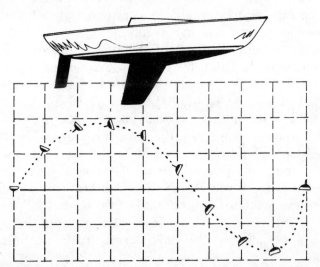

An ultra-light skimming dish of a boat may be fast around the buoys, but
with a limit of positive stability of only 110 degrees, it is an unsafe and
inappropriate design type for offshore sailing.

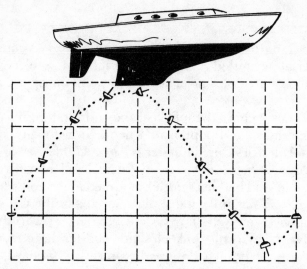

A moderate racer-cruiser with adequate ballast and a seakindly hull form will not win many buoy races but will be a comfortable and fast coastal cruiser and offshore voyager. With a limit of positive stability of 139 degrees, the design type provides a good margin of safety.

A narrow, deep and heavily ballasted cruising boat or a style with a limit of positive stability of 180 degrees will be slow through the water but provides maximum safety in rough weather as well as the ability to carry enormous amounts of stores and gear for long-distance cruising.

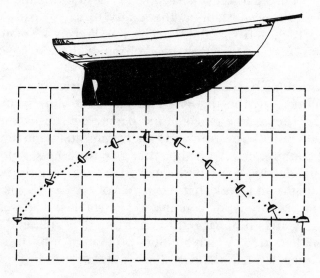

ordinary strength and forming abilities of fiberglass construction.
The material permitted imaginative designers to seek new ways to
make sailboats go fast, and new ways to combine speed and comfort.

The concepts behind the split keel and rudder design type gained
even more renown and popularity when Olin Stephens created the
successful America's Cup defender *Intrepid*. Unlike her competitors
in that season, *Intrepid* had a stubby fin keel and a bustle under the
after quarters, and had her rudder mounted at the end of the bustle
well aft. *Intrepid* was unbeatable. The success of the Cal 40 and of
Intrepid opened many designers' and builders' eyes to the performance advantages of the fin keel, spade rudder design type. It was
not long after that such designs became the standard, both for
modern cruising boats and the racing fleet.

There is little argument today that the split keel and rudder
configuration produces faster boats than configurations of the more
traditional type. If speed is the first prerequisite in a boat, then
lightness, minimum wetted surface and a spade rudder–fin keel
design is the way to go. Yet, for those who will be sailing in conditions other than pure drag racing around the buoys, there are other
considerations that must go into the selection of the right boat. The
sailor who is contemplating sailing long distances along a coast or
making offshore passages must look for design qualities that enhance seaworthiness, stability, the ability to carry loads of gear,
water and fuel, and the ability to be handled by a small—often
two-person—crew, as well as speed through the water (see chart
page 57).

The work done by the Joint Committee on Safety from Capsizing
is a monument to the thought that has gone into yacht design
during the 1980s. The outcome has been a consensus among the
leaders in naval architecture and race organization and among the
leading boat builders. At the beginning of the 1990s, sailors looking for suitable, safe boats in which to go to sea inherit the benefit of
all the thought and work that has taken place. New boats coming
onto the market are being conceived to be stable in bad weather, to
be seakindly and to be rigged for shorthanded sailing. Safety, although not heralded by boat builders' promotion or by the sailors, is
the big winner. And, as the IOR slowly fades away to be replaced by

COMPARISONS OF LIMITS OF POSITIVE STABILITY

	Displacement	Beam	LPS
LH 50	52,435 lbs.	13.38'	114°
Swan 46	37,247 lbs.	14.62'	107°
Cambria 44	36,834 lbs.	13.80'	110°
Mason 43	30,990 lbs.	11.26'	117°
C&C 41 (CB)	22,475 lbs.	13.07'	113°
J/40 (wing keel)	21,047 lbs.	10.42'	118°
Little Harbor 38	27,729 lbs.	12.09'	109°
Tartan 372	18,826 lbs.	9.70'	119°
Beneteau 35S5	13,292 lbs.	9.40'	109°
Catalina 27	7,433 lbs.	7.99'	121°

The calculated limits of positive stability for the 10 boats above is derived from the IMS certificate. The numbers indicated here give a theoretical capsize angle. Because the volume of the cabin and coach roof and the negative volume of the cockpit have not been factored into the formula, the numbers generated by the IMS will consistently read low.

the IMS, sailors around the world will find increasingly that boats brought to them by designers and builders conform to the latest and best thinking in the safety-at-sea category.

CONSTRUCTED FOR SAFETY

The world of sailing—both racing and cruising—experienced an explosion in the late 1960s and 1970s. That explosion continues today, although the roar has become muted over time. During those two decades, a vast number of boats were brought to the market to serve the fast-growing ranks of new sailors. The pace of design and construction was furious. And, as the explosion took place, no single regulating body was able to step forth and assign standards for boats that would set minimum levels—minimum scantlings—that would ensure safe, seaworthy construction.

Yet it is the construction of our boats, the very integrity of the hulls in which we sail, that separates us from the cold waves, from the deep water and from a survival situation. And in hull construction there are several basics a prospective sailor and boat owner should look for to satisfy himself that he and his crew will be setting out in a boat built suitably to the type of sailing ahead.

Lloyd's of London has for years been the largest broker of marine insurance for both commercial and private vessels. As an insurer, Lloyd's developed a set of standards for commercial shipping that was used worldwide by naval architects and shipbuilders. In the same fashion, Lloyd's also developed a set of standards for the construction of pleasure yachts, yachts which it would insure.

The highest Lloyd's certification for a yacht is called Lloyd's A1. Such a certification means that the hull and deck of a yacht have been built to Lloyd's highest standards, and that a Lloyd's surveyor or inspector has been present at critical junctures of the building process. While Lloyd's has other levels of certification, the only one seen in yacht construction is A1. For obvious reasons, no boat builder would build, or advertise the fact that he was building, boats to a lesser standard.

While the Lloyd's standards have proven useful for the consumer, the standards also have suffered from random use and from missing the major technological developments in fiberglass construction. Most builders of pleasure sailing craft do not register with Lloyd's, nor do they adhere strictly to Lloyd's standards. This is largely because the builders of modern production and custom sailing boats are years ahead of the Lloyd's standards in the development and understanding of composite fiberglass construction techniques.

For example, it was only in 1986, in the year preceding the Australian defense of the America's Cup, that Lloyd's sanctioned the use of coring materials in a fiberglass hull. This addition to the construction standards was brought about by the New Zealand challenger group and designers Bruce Farr and Ron Holland, who worked closely with Lloyd's to develop truly modern standards for hull construction. At the time, all America's Cup yachts had to be built to Lloyd's standards. All, in that generation, were built of aluminum. But the New Zealanders, leading the world in fiberglass construction technology, saw an advantage in building their challenger of composite materials. *Kiwi Magic*, as the New Zealand 12-

meter was known, proved herself to be extremely fast. Only the experience and wiles of Dennis Conner, sailing the aluminum *Stars & Stripes*, stopped the "plastic fantastic" 12-meter from New Zealand from taking the Cup away from the Australians.

Today Lloyd's offers builders, designers and boat owners conservative standards for boat construction. A boat that meets the A1 certification will, by definition, be built like a brick privy. Such a craft is the type you may want if you are meandering about coral atolls or heading off to areas where you are liable to find brash ice floating across your anchorage.

However, the sailor who is interested in the leading edge of hull and deck construction will find that the builders are still ahead of the insurers when it comes to fabricating sophisticated cored composite structures.

An American organization that has filled the need for sound basic standards for yacht construction is the American Bureau of Shipping (ABS). The ABS, based in New York, has long been a world leader in the commercial field and a rival of Lloyd's for authority among shipbuilders and commercial surveyors. Only recently, because of the U.S. Naval Academy's need for new sail-training sloops, has the ABS come to grips with the issue of standardizing hull specifications for modern sailing yachts.

The first commercial production sailing boat to be built with the ABS plaque on its bulkhead is the new Annapolis 44, built by Tillotson-Pearson in Rhode Island. The 44-foot sloop, designed by James McCurdy, is a moderate-displacement fin-keeler that rates satisfactorily under the IMS, has a solid offshore rig, a pleasant cockpit that will protect the crew from the weather, and a level of construction and detailing that would make any offshore sailor feel comfortable. Premiering in 1989, the Annapolis 44 set a standard for American-built boats and led the ABS into the world of yacht design, specifications and construction.

Whether a boat is built to Lloyd's or ABS standards is entirely at the discretion of the builder. For quite some time, selective owners who have sought not only the best in their boat but the best in their insurance have had their vessels built to Lloyd's A1 standards. In the early 1990s, many of those boat buyers and those building custom boats will use the new ABS standards instead. In fact, the ABS standards may lead the way, as they have been written by experts who understand the fast-changing world of composite cored fiberglass construction.

Although there is no single governing body offering final standards and a seal of approval for modern production sailboats, the American Boat and Yacht Council (ABYC), a volunteer organization, writes exacting specifications for boat systems and construction details. The ABYC offers yacht designers and boat builders sound, fundamental standards for wiring and electrical configurations, plumbing, engine installations, exhaust systems, hull-to-deck-joint details and much more.

Following ABYC standards is not compulsory for any boat manufacturer, but most use the ABYC standards as a matter of course. The reasons most follow the ABYC lead are simple: Standardization greatly simplifies the commissioning process for boat dealers; standardization offers designers and builders a constant and effective method for analyzing costs in construction; and, finally, adhering to the ABYC standards offers some protection from liability claims against a product.

None of the organizations that set standards for recreational boating have the authority to enforce them. There are many boats available on the market built in the absence of either Lloyd's or ABS inspectors, and without the guidance of the ABYC standards. If you are seriously considering taking your boat and family and crew offshore, then you owe it to yourself and to those who sail with you to inquire into the standards used in the construction of your boat. And, while you may make a decision on a suitable vessel on merits other than the standards to which it was built, it would be wise to check with your insurance agent prior to purchasing a vessel to see if your judgment of quality and value adds up to a vessel that is also insurable.

In hull and deck construction there are some fundamental qualities that mark the difference between a boat designed for safe sailing and a boat that has not been so designed. The following list of questions may be of assistance when you are assessing a boat for safe sailing and extended cruising.

The Keel

Is the keel made of lead? If so, and if it is fastened to the exterior of the hull, have the keel bolts been well positioned and secured in the lead structure?

Is the keel iron? If so, is rust present? Is the keel-hull joint showing separation due to a build-up of rust? Has the iron keel been etched with acid to prevent rust and then coated with an epoxy coating to prohibit further oxidization?

Is the keel a fin? Is the hull robustly reinforced at the keel-hull joint? Do keel bolts pass through strengthening stringers? Are the keel bolts accessible for tightening? Is the keel bedded in a suitable compound, such as 3M's 5200?

Does the keel have wings? Are they cast integrally, or are they bolted into place?

Is the keel encased in the fiberglass hull? Is the hull well protected from grounding damage? Is the ballast secured in place with fiberglass or some other permanent composite construction?

Is there a centerboard in the keel? Can the centerboard be serviced without destroying the keel? Is the centerboard cavity or trunk completely watertight? Does the centerboard have stoppers to keep it from banging against the keel in sloppy weather? Will the centerboard float? Will it bend, preventing raising it, in bad weather?

Is the rudder attached to the keel? Is the heel fitting robust? Are the pintles and gudgeons bolted to the keel, or are they glassed in place? Is the propeller in an aperture? Is the aperture large enough for a larger propeller?

The Rudder

Is the rudder separate from the keel? Does it have a skeg to prevent collision damage? Is there a suitable heel fitting for the skeg-hung rudder?

Is the rudder a spade rudder? Is it balanced? Is the rudder post robust and of a material that will not deteriorate, such as stainless steel? Are metal strengthening plates welded to the rudder post

The integrity of the hull, rudder and keel is the single most important safety factor. Before buying a boat, assess carefully whether the boat's basic construction is suitable to the uses you will put the boat to.

inside the rudder? Is the through-hull for the rudder post heavily built and sealed with a watertight stuffing box or another suitable arrangement?

Is the rudder attached to the keel? Are the pintles and gudgeons fabricated of suitable noncorrosive materials and then bonded electrically to the hull-bonding system? Is the rudder fitted with a heel fitting that is robust? Can it be removed if it is necessary to repair the rudder? Can the propeller shaft be removed without taking off the rudder?

The Hull

Is the hull fiberglass? Has it been laid up to ABS or Lloyd's standards? Has the laminate been built by hand, or was the laminate created with a chopper gun? Was the hull allowed to cure in the mold until the resin had fully kicked? Is the resin resistant to osmotic blistering, like vinylester or epoxy resins? Has a barrier coat of resin been applied below the waterline? Have unidirectional or other strengthening glass fibers been used in stress areas, such as at the chain plates? Does the hull have stringers running fore and aft to strengthen the glass laminate? Are core samples taken while through-hulls were being installed available for inspection?

Is the hull a cored composite construction? Is the coring material of a type approved by ABS or Lloyd's? Has the coring material been fared and filled with epoxy putty prior to coating with glass laminate? Are areas of stress, such as at the hull-keel attachment or at chain plates, cored with solid materials and reinforced?

Is the hull fabricated of steel or aluminum? Has the metal been coated to prevent corrosion? Have zincs been provided to ward off electrolysis? Is the entire hull and engineering bonded adequately and is there a way to ground the hull easily? Have compatible bottom paints been chosen to prevent galvanic corrosion? Are through-hulls and sea cocks of a material compatible with the hull material? Are dissimilar metals, such as steel and bronze, well insulated from each other by a nonconductive material?

Is the hull unsinkable? Have watertight compartments been built in integrally? Can sizable sections of the boat be closed off with watertight doors?

The Through-Hull Fittings

How many through-hulls does the boat have? How many are below the waterline? Are the through-hulls of high quality materials such as bronze or delrin? Can all through-hulls be closed quickly and easily with strong, well-greased sea cocks? Have sea cocks been bonded electrically to the hull-bonding system to prevent galvanic corrosion? Are the through-hulls of a cast metal? Have they been inspected for flaws or cracks?

Are all through-hulls attached to appropriate sea cocks? Are those sea cocks approved by ABS or Lloyd's? Are there any unsuitable steel gate-valves fitted? Are the sea cocks operable? Are wood plugs fitted at each sea cock to plug the through-hull should the sea cock break?

The Hull-Deck Joint

In a fiberglass hull, has a wide flange been provided for mating the hull with the deck molding? Is that flange horizontal or vertical? How has the joint been bonded together? Has a strong, flexible adhesive bedding compound, such as 3M's 5200, been used? Has the deck been bolted to the hull at no more than six-inch intervals? Are the bolts stainless steel and large? Is the toe rail an integral part of the hull-deck joint? Has a sturdy backing plate been provided for all bolts in the joint?

In a fiberglass hull, has the hull-deck joint been fiberglassed together with resin and glass? Has the fiberglassing been done on both the inside and outside of the joint to prevent water from seeping into the joint? Is the toe rail bolted through the joint? If so, is it well bedded and bolted down with stainless-steel bolts of an appropriate size and with appropriate backing plates?

The Deck, Cockpit and Cabin Top

Does the whole deck area have an open and workable arrangement? Are the decks formed with a nonskid pattern or covered with a material such as Tread Master? Will water run off the decks quickly? Are there any built-in tripping spots on deck? Does the

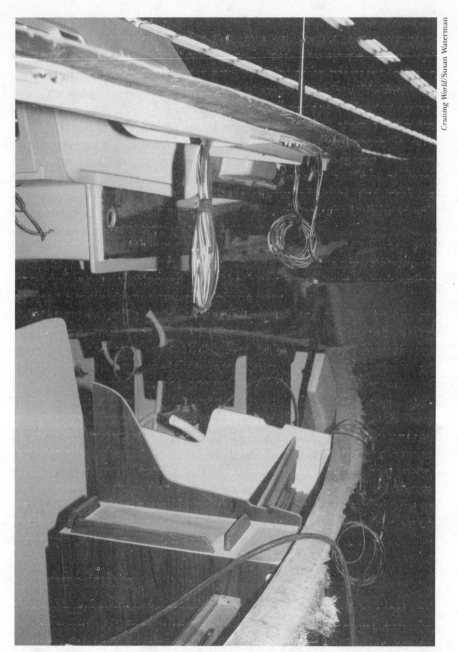

Critical in the construction of any sailing boat is the hull-to-deck joint. The joint should be heavily built and should be fastened together with heavy bolts and sealed with a high-grade marine adhesive.

deck have applied teak on it? If so, is the teak fastened securely to the deck below and bedded in an appropriate bedding compound? Can water migrate beneath the teak? Have all deck fittings been installed with suitable bedding compound and backed up with sturdy backing plates?

Is the cockpit secure from wind and weather? Are lockers provided with positive latches and tight rubber seals to prevent water from leaking below? Has the cockpit been laid out for shorthanded sailing, with either the main sheet or jib sheets near the helmsman? Are the cockpit drains large and protected by a screen to prevent fouling? Will a filled cockpit drain quickly? Is there a bridge deck or companionway hatch designed to prevent water in the cockpit from flooding below decks? Is there a large bilge pump handy to the helmsman and crew?

Does the boat have lifelines? Are they single or double? Can the pelican hooks at the gates be locked with positive latches? Are the stanchions tall enough for the crew? Are the stanchions bolted through the deck and fitted with sturdy backing plates? Are stanchions and the stanchion bases attached with a bolt or set screw?

Is the cabin top heavily constructed and reinforced at its juncture with the deck? Could it withstand the force of a boarding sea? Are handholds provided so crew members can move fore and aft while always maintaining a grip? Can sails be handled from the mast and foredeck safely by one person? Can a reef be tied into the mainsail either from the cockpit or from the mast without undue exposure of the crew to waves and weather? Are there sufficient handholds and safety harness clip-ons to enable a crew member forward of the cockpit always to maintain a solid touch with the boat? Are portholes solid and small enough to withstand a breaking wave? Can cabin-top hatches be securely dogged down from the interior? Is the deck of the cabin top nonskid?

The Rig

Have the designer and builder specified mast sections and rigging size appropriate for your intended use of them? Has the rig been set up correctly, with the mast in a vertical column, the spreaders cocked just slightly upwards (bisecting the angle formed by the shroud)? Are the turnbuckles and spreader ends taped or otherwise padded so they don't chafe on sails, ankles and lines? Are all shrouds of stainless steel, either rod or 1-by-19 wire? Have toggles been fitted between the turnbuckles and chain plates to permit flexing of the rig? Have the swagings and terminals been checked for cracks? Is the boat rigged to fly storm canvas, a trisail on its own track on the mainmast and a spitfire jib on the headstay with its own sheeting points?

Is the mast stepped on deck? If so, has a robust compression post been fitted between the mast step on deck and the keel? Has the on-deck mast step been configured to withstand pumping in the rig in rough seas and high winds? Is the deck watertight where masthead wiring passes through to instruments below decks?

Is the mast stepped on the keel? Have the hull and keel-hull joint been reinforced to withstand the compression of the mast? Does the mast step provide a secure anchor for the foot of the mast to prevent it from shifting when the rig pumps in bad weather? Is the deck reinforced at the partners, where the mast passes through the deck, to prevent cracking and damage when the mast does shift? Is the mast wedged securely in place with either rubber or spruce wedges cut to size and fitted tightly? Is a mast boot fitted to prevent water from flowing below decks at the partners?

THE SECTION ABOVE does not cover every aspect of a boat's construction, but does strive to call your attention to those features in a boat that are most germane to the overall seaworthiness of the vessel. You may find it useful, when assessing a new boat or when equipping your own boat for longer cruises, to examine the overall strength, quality and condition of the boat as objectively as possible.

Understanding how a boat has been engineered, from the lamination schedule—fiberglass and resin components—of the hull, to the way the hull and deck are joined, to the specifics of how the keel, rudder and rig have been conceived and executed, will enable you to judge how suitable a certain boat is to your purposes. It is unfair and perhaps unwise to generalize about what is a good boat and what is not. Both designers and builders tend to stay a step ahead of those who develop standards to regulate the construction of sailing boats. Yet safety demands that certain tried-and-true elements be employed in the creation of a good vessel for the sea, and the Lloyd's, ABS and ABYC standards are built upon those elements.

FIVE RULES FOR CHOOSING A SAFE BOAT

An adage among boat brokers and dealers runs: The happiest days of a sailor's life are the day he buys his new boat and the day he sells his old boat. In between lie the years of sailing, cruising, racing and boat ownership. For most of us, the adage misses the mark. The real pleasure is found in the pure joy of owning a sound, seaworthy vessel. And the ultimate pleasure in a boat comes at the end of a good offshore run, when, with land in sight, with navigation spot on, with gear and crew in good shape, the skipper and owner can say a quiet word of thanks to the stout, able ship that carried him through to a safe landfall.

Finding the right boat for you is not a subject that can be addressed in a general survey of safety at sea. But it is fair to lay down some broad parameters, beyond the more specific categories outlined above, that may prove useful in selecting the proper sailing boat for you and your family and friends to take to sea. These are the Five Rules:

Rule One: Know How You Will Use the Boat

All modern sailing boats available on the market have been built and designed to fulfill certain general requirements of the owner. The Westsail 32, which weighs more than a J-40, was never intended to be a daysailer on a landlocked bay. The purpose of the boat was and is to roam the world, downwind, in the trade winds. It would be folly to ask a Westsail 32 to beat regularly to windward in a light breeze. In fact, it would be madness to expect such a boat to carry her crew any long distance to windward in any breeze. The boat will carry her crew clumsily off a lee shore in just about anything, and for that the boat deserves credit. But her purpose and the trade she will enter into most profitably is bobbing like a cork before the winds of the tropics.

If you do not seriously plan to drift westward with the trade winds, then a boat such as a Westsail 32 is probably not for you.

When laying down parameters for choosing the right sailing boat, the safe and able boat, it is important to know what you will really need the boat to do. Will you be cruising only during weekends, and will you have to be back on Sunday night no matter what? Will you have a week or two to take off during the sailing season? How far will you go? And will the prevailing wind be against you one way or the other? Or both?

All of these factors will come to bear on how you select the right boat for you and your family.

Another consideration should be given passing thought as well. How do you and your family and friends think about your time away from home? There are some who go sailing to get away from all that smacks of home, away from the phone, the complexities of shoreside life, our dependency on comforts and services. For these sailors, the boat is like a cabin in the woods. It should be simple, plain, and involve a minimum of maintenance and a minimum of worry. For such sailors, a simple, basic boat offers the one thing they cannot find ashore: simplicity next to nature.

For those who feel the need to shower twice a day, who require ice in their drinks and carpet under their feet, a boat is a very different expression of style and use. Using a boat as a waterfront condo, as opposed to a cabin in the woods, requires a different technological level aboard, more complex systems and someone at hand to maintain those systems.

When thinking of a suitable boat to fill your cruising needs, it might well be foolish to think of sailing a floating condominium very far offshore without first having a good look at the construction of the boat and having run the numbers on stability. But if you never intend to sail out of sight of land, then it is prudent to select a boat that fills the comfort needs first and seakeeping needs second. A floating, sailing condo has much to recommend it over the fixed, shoreside variety.

If you are looking for a boat in which to sail far and wide, then you must know if you will be sailing often to windward, often downwind or often both of the above. You must know how often you like to pull into gas docks and watering holes, how often you will need to replenish fresh foods, and how much deck cargo—life raft, dinghies, extra sails and so on—you will have to carry when crossing open stretches of water.

Knowing how you will use your boat involves knowing what your sailing and cruising style is going to be. If you fool yourself—Hell, of course I'm sailing around the world!—while in fact you and your family have no intention of doing that, then you will end up with the wrong boat for the coastal gunkholing you end up enjoying. Be honest. Don't buy a dream. Buy the right boat for the real sailing and cruising you will be doing. If that sailing pattern changes, then it will be time to change boats.

Rule Two: Know Where You Will Be Sailing

Rule Two follows closely on the heels of Rule One, yet it has an important difference. As Rule One says, be honest about where you plan to sail and how you plan to use the boat. Otherwise you can be stuck with a trade wind cork that wants to float you to Bali, while you are beating, without much success, into your prevailing head wind.

Beyond the simple requirement to be honest, however, every sailor looking for a new sailboat, a new cruising boat or club racer, should first take a long, hard look at the charts for the areas in which he or she will be sailing.

If you will be sailing out of Cape Cod and plan to venture no farther than Cuttyhunk and Nantucket, then you will be hard pressed to find any water under your keel deeper than 30 feet. Most of the time the water you'll want to sail in will be shallower than 15 feet. And the best anchorages will require depths of less than five feet.

So, if that's your sailing region, deciding to buy a boat that draws seven feet—even though it has great offshore talent—would be an exercise in frustration.

Too much draft is always a concern, particularly for sailors on the East Coast, where several of the best cruising areas are noted for their lack of water: southern New England, Long Island Sound,

Chesapeake Bay, Albermarle and Pamlico Sound, the Florida Keys, the Bahamas. If you can draw a circle around the areas you are likely to sail and not leave the shallows just listed, then it may make sense to look for a boat that offers shoal draft.

Weather patterns are the other major concern when selecting a boat to match a sailing region. In the Pacific Northwest, pilothouse designs have become popular because sailors out of Seattle and Vancouver know they will face both rain and cool winds. In Florida and southern California, sun is the major concern, so Bimini tops and ample ventilation must play a role in selecting a boat for the region.

Draft and the type of weather that will likely be faced should be major decision points in selecting a vessel for sailing with family and friends. Understanding these two aspects will lead to choosing the right boat for the region and for your use of it in that climate. That boat, the right boat, will be the safest boat you can choose.

Rule Three: Understand a Boat's Designed Purpose

All boats are compromises. Production boats that are sold on a mass scale must be designed to appeal to the widest possible audience. Limited-production boats tend to be designs that fill one special niche in the market, boats that speak to one type of sailor with one special type of sailing need.

Modern sailing boats under 50 feet tend to group themselves into two basic categories: those that are designed to be as light and fast as possible, which have evolved from racing boats, and those that are conceived as load-carriers, which have evolved from the wood-built work boats of years gone by.

It is important to keep the two ideas separate. If you intend to carry two tons of personal belongings, 200 gallons of fuel and 200 gallons of water, as well as three months' supply of canned goods, you would do yourself a disservice to try to accomplish the task in a light-displacement boat that was designed to sail light and sail quickly.

And the converse is equally true. Those who intend to sail only along the coast and near to home, who plan to race in the weeknight beer can races and might, once a year, venture off for two or three weeks on an extended coastal cruise, would be better served by a light fin-keeler than by a dowdy load-carrier. When coastal sailing, every time you meet another boat on your relative course is a race. It's important to admit this. Why choose to sail slowly, to carry four times as much fuel as you need, to trundle about vast amounts of unnecessary stores and equipment, when you could be slipping through the water like a killer whale?

Modern sailing boats can do either, but few or none can do both. When you are puzzling over the parameters you require in a boat, it is important to match a boat's designed purpose—the inherent compromise—with your own purpose when out sailing.

Rule Four: Know a Boat's Numbers

More often than not, a sailor will select a boat in which to spend the next few years enjoying the water, cruising, racing and occasionally sailing offshore by simply knowing in the seat of his pants what's right and what's not. That system, vague as it may be, has worked, on and off, for years. But there is a better way.

In this chapter we have discussed stability, capsize coefficients and other fundamental numbers that can be derived from a boat's specifications and lines. Although it may not be necessary for a skipper to study these numbers, it may be prudent.

The stability range of a hull, as calculated from the IMS measurements, will give you a very clear idea how a boat will perform in storm conditions. You will also get a good reading on how you will have to handle the boat in given situations, such as running off, heaving-to, or lying ahull.

The Capsize Screening Number, derived with the formula given on p. 53 will give you a quick and simplified fix on the boat's inherent stability, its likelihood of capsizing and its initial stability. Although only a general number, the Capsize Screening Number can prove useful when comparing different boats.

Rule Five: Evaluate a Boat Dispassionately

At the beginning of this chapter we discussed briefly the problem most boat owners have with their boats. We all think our boats are beautiful, unless the boat has been for sale for a year. And we have heard from friends, brokers and others that we will know the right next boat, the boat that will take us farther than ever before, the safe, seaworthy vessel of our dreams, when we see it. It will be love at first sight.

Often that's just what happens.

But once the pangs have hit, once the mind has been switched off by desire, once the decision has been made irrevocably, then it is time to take a long walk. Or a cold shower. Or have a sobering chat with a nonsailing friend.

Once the right boat seems to have appeared, the time has arrived to take a long, dispassionate look at what the boat is really all about. The time has come to inspect the keel and rudder, the fiberglass construction and the core samples from the through-hulls. It is time to look at the rig and assess, frankly, if it is of a size commensurate with your needs for strength, durability and safety.

A boat that fits your sailing requirements is a thing of real beauty. But it is critical, before you get carried away on the magic carpet, that you stop and look at the boat with a cold eye. Despite its beauty, in the end it will either be a safe and sound vessel for you and your crew or it won't. If it is safe, well constructed, soundly fitted out and ready for the rigors of the sea, then its beauty will be a delightful bonus.

But safety must come first.

Chapter 3

SAFETY STANDARDS SET BY THE PROS

International Organizations
Coast Guard Requirements
The Rules of the Road
The Offshore Racing Council Special
    Regulations

FOR A DEVOTED sailor there may be no more enjoyable time on the water than when sailing in a well-fitted boat with a competent crew against difficult but not especially dangerous weather. Feeling a stout vessel heave and buck as it surges ahead with the sails humming in the wind is exhilarating. Knowing that those with you are experienced, well prepared and ready to face difficulties is encouraging and comforting. And having a vessel that has been equipped with gear designed to meet normal sailing requirements and any form of emergency can give one a measure of confidence.

Aboard such a vessel, setting off from land is a pleasure; sailing a distance, even through poor weather and high winds, is a challenge gamely met; and making landfall at the other end is a victory worth toasting with a glass of the ration.

Safety on the water requires a knowledge of the law, an understanding of the best standards of seamanship and constant vigilance.

As we discussed in Chapter 1, the difference between a well-prepared boat and an ill-prepared one can make the difference between a successful sailing passage and an unsuccessful one. Experience of the sea over the years has taught seamen and sailors what works and what does not aboard coastal and oceangoing sailboats. For those with experience, readying a boat and equipping it with the right gear has become second nature.

However, for those preparing themselves and their boats for a first adventure there are basic standards for safety that have been set by those with the vast experience to know the difference between what is right and what is not.

The goal of every skipper is to prepare himself and his vessel to avoid the small problems aboard that can lead to the larger disaster which can threaten the boat and the crew. The basic safety regulations and practices described below are designed to help in that preparation. These are standards of preparation set by the pros.

THE INTERNATIONAL ORGANIZATIONS

The safety regulations and standards that we will discuss below are the work of several American and international organizations. Long before the Iron Curtain began to fall away, long before the nations of East and West began to seek common ground in earnest, the seafarers of the world knew their lives depended on the goodwill of all seamen.

Seafaring tradition predates many of the national and territorial arrangements that make up the modern world. Seafarers have, in their own way, formed a separate nation on the high seas. All at sea for pleasure or commerce share a common purpose: to sail safely, directly between ports, and to do so with a minimum risk to life, ships and cargo. And in the face of adversity, seafaring tradition has always maintained that all ships must come to the aid of a ship in distress if at all possible.

At sea, we look after each other as nowhere else in the world.

In the United States, the U.S. Coast Guard, through its Boating Safety Office, is responsible for the well-being and safety of recreational sailors and boat owners. The Coast Guard also plays a regulating role in defining minimum standards for safety equipment to be carried on pleasure boats. As of the 1990s, the Boating Safety Office in the Commandant's Office in Washington, D.C., has been trimmed to a barebones staff. Always under pressure from Congress and the executive branch to contain costs, and under equal pressure to fight and win the war against drug smugglers, the Coast Guard has shifted priorities from boating safety to defense and interdiction. While the recreational boat owner and sailor is the loser in the trade-off, there remains in place a working Boating Safety Office and sound standards for safety that all who go out in boats must follow.

Internationally, the International Maritime Organization (IMO) forms a governing body, under the umbrella of the United Nations, that negotiates between countries to mandate or recommend, in some cases, standards and codes covering the rules of the road on the high seas, maritime safety, ocean pollution standards and much more. The IMO as we know it today was founded in 1948. Yet the organization's roots go back to 1914, when an international committee was formed to assess the loss of the Titanic.

The IMO was responsible for negotiating and finally promulgating the International Regulations for Preventing Collisions at Sea, which were published in 1972 and went into effect in July 1977. The rules, which are known as the '72 COLREGS, were adopted by the U.S. Congress in 1977, thereby requiring all U.S. flag vessels to adhere to the rules when outside the established lines of demarcation. Such lines will be noted on your charts.

The IMO COLREGS were amended in 1981 to add a number of alterations and improvements. The amendments went into effect in 1983. For accurate regulations you must refer to rules published in 1984 or after.

The U.S. Congress, with the help of the 50 states, the Army Corps of Engineers and the Coast Guard, is responsible for formulating the Inland Rules of the Road. These rules, once divided among Inland Rules, Western River Rules and Great Lakes Rules, are the result of more than 20 years of bickering, infighting and lobbying. The ratification of the '72 COLREGS by Congress spurred a period of constructive activity at home, which parted the seas of lobbyists, pork-barrel politics and regional special interests to form a unified Inland Rules system. The rules, as legislated by Congress, went into effect in 1981 for most of the country and in March of 1983 for the Great Lakes.

The Inland Rules and the International Rules both contain 38 rules and four annexes, which are similar in both content and the form in which they were written. The Inland Rules also contain a fifth annex which covers situations special to navigation in U.S. waters.

The International Maritime Organization has played an important and wide-ranging role in standardizing regulations, codes and recommendations for ships on the high seas and, through local legislation, in many countries of the world. For the sailor, however, one of the most important IMO contributions to his well-being has come from the International Convention for Safety of Life at Sea, known as

SOLAS. Unlike Coast Guard requirements, the recommendations for safety gear and standards issued by SOLAS are not compulsory. SOLAS has provided standards for everything from flares to life preservers, and the standards tend to be extremely high.

At the recreational level, the sport of sailing in the United States is governed by the United States Yacht Racing Union (USYRU), which has approximately 25,000 members across the country. The union, although primarily dedicated to overseeing small-boat racing and establishing fair racing protocols and rules for sailors on the race-course, has a wide-ranging role to play in sailing. The USYRU Boating Safety Committee has taken an active role in the analysis of modern yacht design, safety gear and techniques, and in providing education to the general sailing public on these and other topics. The Joint Committee on Safety from Capsizing was an effort that linked the USYRU's safety committee with the Society of Naval Architects and Marine Engineers. Their Final Report, discussed in Chapter 2, is a seminal work in the field of safety at sea in recreational boats.

The USYRU is a national organization and sends delegates to the International Yacht Racing Union (IYRU), which is the worldwide regulating body for the sport of sailing and ocean racing. The IYRU sets protocols and standards for the sport of sailing as a consensus of sailing nations worldwide.

While the USYRU and IYRU are primarily focused on racing, safety is always a foremost concern. Working in league with the IYRU, the Offshore Racing Council (ORC), has become the oracle for standards of equipment and safety for ocean-sailing boats around the world. The ORC's publication *Special Regulations Governing Offshore Racing* can be considered the best—if the most conservative—guide to equipping and preparing a vessel safely for a journey or race at sea.

In the best seafaring tradition, the governmental organizations, the international organizations and the recreational groups have all contributed fundamentally to the safety of mariners at sea. Each organization will be more than cooperative should you wish to find out more about how it functions and how its standards have been established.

COAST GUARD REQUIREMENTS

All sailors who go out on the water, no matter how large or small their boats, are required by law to carry minimum safety equipment. These requirements can be enforced by the Coast Guard, should you be boarded for a random safety inspection, or by state boating-safety officers or by a locality's marine police. Should you fail to carry the minimum safety equipment, you can be cited by the boarding officers and either given a warning or, in the worst cases, fined.

While carrying the minimum safety equipment is the law, the standards set by the Coast Guard for the general boating population are no more than common sense. In fact, complying with the law is only the very first step in the process of preparing a boat and its crew to sail any distance along the coast or offshore.

Life Preservers

Until 1988, the ordinary life preserver was known in Coast Guard parlance as the "personal flotation device." These were then divided into four types. Since 1988, the names of the various types have changed, but the basic requirements for the vests have remained the same.

Every vessel over 16 feet in length is required to carry a wearable life jacket for every person on board, plus one throwable flotation device. Boats under 16 feet may carry either a wearable or a throwable flotation device for each person—throwable meaning the old Type IV devices, which include cockpit cushions and life rings.

Wearable flotation devices are not all alike. The Coast Guard has arrived at three different classifications, each designed to describe a life jacket suitable for various uses.

The Offshore Life Jacket (Type I). Intended for serious sailors, those who will be heading offshore or making long coastal runs, the Offshore Life Jacket must have at least 22 pounds of inherent buoyancy. The jacket is designed to hold an unconscious person upright in the water in a position that should keep his head free of the water and allow him to breathe. Although bulky, the offshore jacket provides the best protection for most sailors.

However, both the Navy and the Coast Guard have determined that their sailors need more protection. Both services mandate that the life jackets worn on deck must have at least 32 pounds of flotation and must have a collar which will turn an unconscious person faceup in the water. If you are determined to carry the ultimate in gear, then Navy-grade 32-pound flotation jackets will be the flotation devices of choice.

The Nearshore Buoyancy Vest (Type II). While this is the most popular style of life jacket for inshore and coastal uses, it is no longer recommended. The nearshore vest must have a minimum buoyancy of 15.5 pounds. The design of the vest will turn most people faceup in the water, although in some cases an unconscious person may not be turned faceup by the vest. The vest will be easy to stow aboard your boat but will be uncomfortable and will get in your way while trying to sail.

The Flotation Aid (Type III). Usually a trim vest or float coat, the flotation aid must provide a minimum of 15.5 pounds of buoyancy. However, the aid will not hold your head clear of the water, nor will it turn an unconscious person faceup. Undoubtedly the most comfortable of the three types of life jackets, the flotation aid may be the most likely to be worn but will also offer the least amount of protection for a person in the water.

Throwable Device (Type IV). This horseshoe ring, or life ring, or cockpit flotation cushion, will be located in your cockpit and is designed to be thrown the instant a person goes over the side. The device must provide a minimum of 16.5 to 18 pounds of buoyancy. A throwable device should not be considered a life preserver or life jacket. However, in an emergency, those left onboard will want one handy to throw quickly to the victim in the water. The ring or cushion should not be worn in the water for any length of time, for it will force the wearer to float facedown.

Hybrid Devices (Type V). In recent years a new category of flotation device has appeared that has found a ready audience among offshore sailors. The hybrid devices are most commonly life preservers of the Mae West type—CO_2-inflated—coupled with a stout safety

The Coast Guard requires that a personal flotation device be carried aboard for each person on the boat. The three "wearable" type are: the Offshore Life Jacket (top) formerly known as Type I; the Nearshore Buoyancy Vest (middle), formerly the Type II; and the Flotation Aid (bottom), formerly the Type III.

harness or float coat. When deflated, these devices must offer a
minimum of 7.5 pounds of buoyancy; when inflated, they must
offer the wearer at least 22 pounds of buoyancy. Although somewhat bulky for everyday wear, the hybrid devices can be worn
comfortably over foul weather jackets and serve double duty for
those on watch. Each device will be rated either Type I, II or III,
clearly marked on the label. It is essential to maintain the cartridges
on these devices and to inspect the flotation chambers periodically
for wear or pinholes.

Sounding Device

In poor visibility, whether at night or in a fog, it is essential that a
boat and its crew have a way of identifying itself with some sort of
sounding device. The Coast Guard mandates the following minimum devices:

Boats under 16 feet: No sounding device required.

Boats 16 to 25 feet: Must carry a horn or whistle (mouth, hand or
power operated) that can be heard for at least half a mile.

Boats 26 to 39 feet: Must carry one bell; must carry a horn or
whistle (mouth, hand or power operated) that can be heard for at
least one mile.

Boats 40 to 65 feet: Must carry one bell; must carry a power
operated horn or whistle that can be heard for at least one mile.

THE REQUIREMENT TO carry horns and bells is mandated not only
by the Coast Guard but also by the International and Inland Rules
of the Road. While the requirement of a horn as a device to signal
maneuvers to other vessels in close quarters will be thought of as
reasonable by most sailors, a bell is often regarded as a vestigial
noisemaker from the days of Captain James Cook. It is wise to
remember that the bell is used primarily to signal one's position at
anchor in poor visibility and when aground—both instances when
you will be glad another vessel can hear you clearly.

Visual Distress Signals

All boats on the water must be equipped with some sort of day and night visual distress signaling device. In boats under 16 feet, these can be one and the same, namely a flashlight that can be operated to send a flashing Morse SOS, as well as to help you find your anchored boat after Happy Hour ashore. There are exceptions to this regulation. You need not carry a day signaling device aboard boats in a race or marine parade, if you are in an open sailboat under 26 feet or if you are in a boat propelled solely by oars. After sunset, however, you *must* carry a night signaling device.

Boats between 16 and 65 feet must carry the following:

By day: an orange flag bearing a black square and a black circle, or three floating orange smoke signals, or three hand-held orange smoke signals.

By night (only): an electric distress light capable of signaling in Morse, such as a flashlight with an on/off button.

By day and night (combination signals): three red parachute flares, or three red meteor (pyrotechnic) flares, or three hand-held red flares, or three red pistol-fired flares. Note: Flares must be dated by the manufacturer. Flares more than three years old will be considered by inspecting safety officers as being out-of-date.

Fire Extinguishers

To combat fires aboard, the Coast Guard mandates that all vessels with inboard engines and all powered vessels over 26 feet carry fire extinguishers. Vessels under 26 feet with enclosed compartments, built-in fuel tanks or other integral areas in which fumes and fuel could collect must also carry fire extinguishers.

Fire extinguishers are delineated by the types of fires they are intended to suppress. A types fight combustible-solids fires; B types fight fires fed by combustible fuels and other flammable fluids; C types are designed for electrical fires. All extinguishers required by the Coast Guard are of the B type. The roman numerals I and II delineate the throw-weight of the extinguishers. Type I contains any of the following: 4 pounds of carbon dioxide; 2 pounds of dry chemical; 2½ pounds of Halon; 1½ gallons of foam. Type II contains 15 pounds of carbon dioxide; or 10 pounds of dry chemical; or 10 pounds of Halon; or 2½ gallons of foam.

The requirements are:

Boats 26 to 39 feet: two B-I; or one B-I and one B-II; or, if a fixed engine-room system is in place, one additional B-I.

Boats 39 to 65 feet: three B-I; or one B-I and one B-II; or, with a fixed system in place, two additional B-I and one additional B-II.

Ventilation

The ability to quickly and safely evacuate flammable gasses from the bilge or engine room of a boat is a key ingredient in the safety of the vessel. The Coast Guard requires all inboard gasoline-powered vessels to be equipped with appropriate systems to ventilate the engine room. The minimum vent duct should be two inches in diameter and should vent through a cowl that is at least three square inches in area. Boats built after 1980 must also be equipped with an electrical blower in the duct system.

Fewer and fewer sailboats are equipped with gas-powered auxiliaries. However, many do have propane stoves aboard, hence the commonsense regulations in place to combat gasoline fires should be adopted voluntarily by all who carry flammables within the hulls of their vessels.

Backfire Flame Arrestor

All inboard gasoline engines must be equipped with a backfire flame arrestor, which will prevent ignited gasoline from escaping from the carburetor and creating an explosion in the engine room.

Oil Discharge Plaques

It is illegal to pump or otherwise discharge oil or petroleum products into the sea. All boats over 26 feet with inboard engines must purchase and display on the engine a plaque that informs all aboard of the law.

Navigation Lights

The COLREGS, the International and Inland Rules of the Road, mandate a standardized system of navigation lights for all vessels operating at night. It is not only necessary to equip your boat with the appropriate running, steaming and anchor lights, but every member of the crew should be familiar with the standards used by commercial vessels in order to avoid collisions while under way.

Under power. All boats under power must carry sidelights, a stern light and a white steaming light shining forward describing the same arc as the sidelights. Boats under 39 feet must show sidelights visible for one mile and a steaming light visible for two miles. Boats between 39 and 65 feet must carry sidelights and a stern light visible for two miles and a steaming light visible for three miles.

Under sail. Boats under 23 feet must carry a white light (flashlight) that can be shown if necessary. Boats between 26 and 39 feet must show sidelights visible for one mile and a stern light visible for two miles. On larger sailing vessels, all three lights must be visible for two miles.

At anchor, all vessels must show a 360-degree anchor light between sunrise and sunset, except in anchorages in which anchor lights have been designated as optional.

THE COAST GUARD requirements for all boats on the water should be considered a beginning point when equipping your boat for the sea. These are the minimum standards any seafarer should meet. The prudent skipper will go a great deal further to equip himself and his craft with equipment designed to provide for the safety of the crew.

RULES OF THE ROAD

The COLREGS, discussed above, are the International and Inland Rules of the Road, formulated by the International Maritime Organization to prevent collisions at sea. Every vessel 39 feet and over must carry a copy of the rules aboard, and every vessel actively sailing along shore or at sea should carry a copy of the rules. The COLREGS are the bible for the safe operation of a boat in any and all encounters with other vessels at sea.

The COLREGS are divided into 38 rules and five annexes. The rules are delineated by general categories. Although promulgated primarily for motorized commercial vessels, the COLREGS cover all the essential rules of the road for all vessels, whether under sail, under power or oar powered.

Part A: General

The first section of the rules lays out the legal framework and defines the general terms used within the rules.

Of particular importance to sailors is Rule 2, which should be considered an essential preamble to understanding and following the rules which follow. Rule 2 stipulates that following the COL-REGS to the letter of the rule does not exonerate a skipper from his responsibility for operating his vessel safely and in a seamanlike fashion. Common sense, in other words, can not be dictated by rules yet must be considered the first requisite for making all judgments when operating a vessel. If, in a collision situation, a skipper would put himself and his boat in danger of grounding by following the normal rules, he must take another appropriate action, dictated by common sense and seamanship, that will avoid the collision and the danger of grounding. The rules provide a uniform guide to the safe operation of a boat. They do not provide all the answers to every situation met while under way.

Part B: Steering and Sailing Rules

Rules 4 through 19 cover the basic rules of the road. These rules are the conventions adopted by sailors worldwide to avoid collisions and to permit different types of craft, from fishing boats to sailboats to commercial freighters and dredges, to share the same waters without danger of incident and collision.

For sailors, the rules that have the most immediate relationship to the ordinary business of sailing and cruising will be familiar. The need to maintain a constant and vigilant lookout (Rule 4) is understood by most navigators. Although the growth of singlehanded sailing and racing has created some notable exceptions to the practice of following this rule, in general sailing, maintaining a watchful eye on the horizon and other traffic in your area is just plain good sense.

How sailing vessels react to each other when they meet and both are under sail is one of the first aspects all sailors study when taking up sailing. Rule 12 covers sailing encounters. Both vessels are required to remain clear, yet the rules define which boat must alter course (the give-way vessel) and which should hold its course (the stand-on vessel). When one boat is on the starboard tack and one is on the port tack, the port-tack vessel must give way. When both boats are on the starboard tack, the boat to windward must give way. When you are sailing on the port tack and cannot determine which tack the approaching vessel is on, assume you are the give-way vessel and alter course appropriately. Lastly, an overtaking vessel must keep clear of a vessel being overtaken.

It is important to remember that when altering course to avoid a collision, the course change must be made in a timely way and must be significant enough to indicate that the give-way vessel is indeed giving way (Rule 16).

For boats and ships under power, the basic premise for avoiding

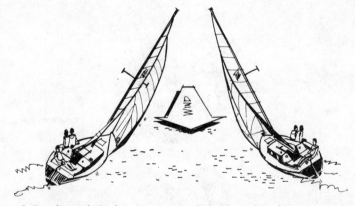

Port and Starboard Rule: In a crossing situation between two sailing vessels, the boat on the starboard tack (wind coming over the starboard side) is the "stand-on" vessel, while the boat on the port tack is the "give-way" vessel.

Windward and Leeward Rule: When two sailing vessels are converging while on the same tack, the leeward boat is the "stand-on" vessel and the windward boat is the "give-way" vessel. The windward boat should tack away or should slow down and steer behind the leeward boat.

Overtaking Vessel Rule: When one boat is overtaking another from behind, the overtaking boat is the "give-way" vessel and the boat being overtaken is the "stand-on" vessel. It is common courtesy for the overtaking boat to sail well to leeward when passing the boat ahead.

collisions is the port-to-port (red-to-red running light) convention as spelled out in Rule 14. In a head-on situation, both vessels are required to alter their courses to starboard, thereby permitting the other vessel to pass to port.

When in a crossing situation (Rule 17, in which the two boats or vessels maintain a constant relative bearing and therefore are on a collision course), the boat that has the other vessel on its starboard side is the give-way vessel and should alter course to avoid a collision. When altering course, the give-way vessel should strive to set a new course that will pass behind the stand-on vessel. The stand-on vessel should hold its course and permit the give-way vessel to demonstrate its intentions by altering course. Also, a sound signal (see Part D below) should be used.

The steering and sailing rules are the internationally accepted means of avoiding collisions and navigating in crowded waters. Although the rules may seem elementary, it is wise for a skipper to review them and to have his crew review them before setting out to do battle with other boats and ships in a crowded waterway.

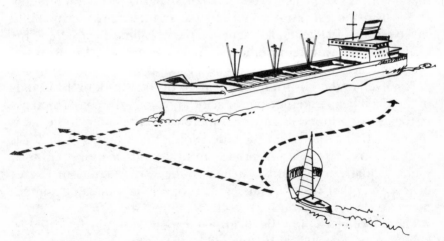

Avoiding Collision: Although a sailing vessel has the right-of-way over a powering vessel at sea, in the confines of a channel or in areas in which a larger vessel may not be able to maneuver, the ship has right-of-way. When two vessels meet, the vessel that has the other vessel on its starboard side is the "give-way" vessel, while the vessel which has the other vessel on its port side is the "stand-on" vessel.

Part C: Lights and Shapes

How a vessel is lighted at night and the solid shapes it flies during the day are the language and code of identification for all boats on the water. Running lights are an integral part of the basic Coast Guard requirements discussed above. Rules 21, 22 and 25 of the COLREGS spell out precisely the design of running lights and the required strength (distance visible) of such lights.

Every boat that intends to sail along a coast or through a busy shipping lane is obliged to make certain that its lights are installed correctly, are in good working condition and are of the type specified for the size of the boat.

To sail safely among the commercial fleets of the world, it is necessary for the skipper and the crew of a sailboat to recognize the lights employed by the widely different types of cargo and fishing boats to be found along a coast at night. Rules 23, 24 and 26 through 31 spell out the various light configurations that must be used in every commercial activity. The experienced sailor will know that it is vital to be able to recognize these lights without hesitation. In most instances, professional sailors, commercial fishermen and cargo seamen follow the rules meticulously. Failing to adhere to the COLREGS lighting requirements can be grounds for dismissal and even legal action against the offending skipper.

However, in the far-flung sailing areas of the world, in the islands of the Caribbean and the South Pacific and along the coasts of many of the less-developed countries, adherence to the letter of the law is the exception rather than the rule. No matter where you sail, it is vital to look for the appropriate running and steaming lights at night. Equally important is a healthy dose of skepticism. Never believe the other vessel has its lights properly lit, nor that its intentions are clear, until you have it safely behind you.

Many modern sailing boats are equipped with masthead lights, known as tricolor lights. If your sailboat is under 20 meters, or less than 65 feet, you have a choice of which running lights to illuminate when under sail at night. You may either light the tricolor at the masthead or light your conventional running lights on deck. Both sets of running lights should never be illuminated at the same time.

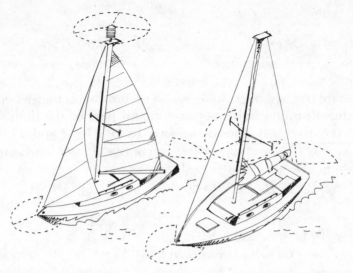

Running Lights: The diagram above shows the lights required for pleasure craft under 65 feet when sailing or steaming at night. Under sail a boat may use either the tricolor or the standard running lights. Under power it must use only the standard running lights.

When motor sailing, the sailboat immediately becomes a power vessel and must use only conventional running lights, plus a steaming light mounted as far forward as possible. This steaming light must be visible through an arc of 225 degrees; in vessels less than 65 feet, it must be visible for three miles, and in vessels under 39 feet it must be visible for two miles.

Unless you regularly use your running lights, you will find that the electrical connections of most standard light installations will corrode rapidly and will require regular maintenance. As a matter of course, it is always prudent to check and weatherproof your running and steaming lights before setting off for an over-nighter.

Part D: Sound and Light Signals

Implicit in the writing of regulations governing the rules of the road at sea and the conduct of vessels in close quarters is the need for those vessels to be able to communicate in a simple and direct manner. Rules 32 through 37 cover the protocol for using sound and sight signals between vessels to alert another skipper to your intentions, present situation and imminent maneuvers.

In discussing the Coast Guard requirements, we mentioned the need to carry a bell and a sounding horn or whistle aboard. Simple procedures for the use of these devices are spelled out in the COL-REGS. A directional light, such as a beam or a high-powered flashlight, may be used at night in the same way a horn or whistle is used in daylight. Here are the signals you must use to announce your intended maneuvers to another vessel:

One short blast: I am altering course to starboard.
Two short blasts: I am altering course to port.
Three short blasts: I am in reverse.
Two long and one short blast: I am going to overtake you on your starboard side.
Two long followed by two short blasts: I am going to overtake you on your port side.

THE VESSEL BEING signaled in a close-quarter situation is obliged to return a signal to confirm to the signaling skipper that the message has been heard and understood. The standard responses are:

When responding to a vessel on a collision course, repeat the signal received and then either hold your course while the other vessel alters his, or alter your course to conform to the intended maneuver.

When responding to an overtaking situation, the overtaken vessel, upon hearing the signal of the overtaking vessel's intentions, should respond by sounding one long, one short, one long and one short blast, in that order.

In any of the above situations and upon hearing a signal that will put either your vessel or another vessel in danger, the correct response is to sound the danger signal.

The danger signal is at least five short, rapid blasts. The danger signal should be repeated as necessary.

Rules 36 and 37 deal with emergency and distress signaling. Distress signals are also covered in more detail in Annex IV of the rules.

The strobe light, which has become common at the mastheads of cruising boats, is considered by the rules to be both a device to attract attention and a device to signal distress. How a strobe is to be used in the two different circumstances is not covered by the rules. However, practice and basic seamanship lead one to make the following observation. A masthead strobe should be turned on if and only if a boat is in immediate danger of a collision with a large commercial vessel. The light will attract the attention of the watch on the bridge and will alert those in command of a possible collision. Once a collision has been averted, the strobe should be switched off.

In more extreme cases, and only when operating within the Inland Rules, a strobe should be used as a distress signal, in the same way you would use a flare or an emergency distress flag. The strobe should be switched on when you have decided that you can no longer manage without outside assistance. Once you have switched on your strobe in distress, should the situation so dictate, you should be prepared to abandon your boat in favor of your rescuer's.

The strobe, while efficient and powerful, is often misused. For example, fishermen off the coast of the Pacific Northwest often will leave a strobe flashing all night as they set their trawls. Such a use of the strobe is a violation of the COLREGS. Although the light may be useful for a fishing fleet striving to stay clear of each other's nets, it also sends a signal to the unwary—the passing freighter, the transient cruising boat—that sailors seek attention and may need assistance. At sea, under the International Rules, the strobe does not signal that you are in distress, but it does require a prompt response by anyone who sees it.

It is vital, therefore, to use the strobe and all distress signals as dictated by the International Rules. To do otherwise is to cry wolf.

Distress signaling at sea, as covered by the COLREGS, offers the seaman a wide variety of methods to attract the attention of passing vessels that might be able to render assistance. Although the rules specify several standard methods, the seaman's aim is to attract attention as quickly as possible and to transmit, by whatever means necessary, the standard message SOS.

Using flags, you can fly the required black circle and square on an orange field, the signals November Charlie; or your American flag or ensign upside down.

With a sounding device, repeated and continuous blasts on a horn, whistle or gong will work, or you can fire a gun at one-minute intervals.

Radio signals include setting off an emergency position-indicating radio beacon (EPIRB) or calling a Mayday via VHF or long-range radio.

Other visual signals include: lighting a flare, either parachute, meteor or hand-held; deploying a smoke signal or dye marker; or, lastly, simply waving your arms up and down in rapid succession.

With a light or sounding device, sending the signal SOS or simply sending repeated short blasts will transmit the distress message. Lastly, illuminating a strobe light will attract attention; a distress situation can then be signaled by other means.

THE COLREGS ARE a set of 38 rules. Their purpose is to prevent collisions at sea and to provide for the safety of mariners on the high seas and on inland waters. The rules are dry and impersonal and may appear to some sailors to formalize what common sense already dictates.

Yet it is important for all sailors concerned with safety aboard their boats to remember that the COLREGS embody the seamanship and wisdom distilled from hundreds of years of seafaring. All sailors are better and safer on the water because of the rules laid down in the COLREGS. Thus it is vitally important that all sailors know the rules, follow them and insist that those who sail as crew be well versed in their content and meaning.

THE OFFSHORE RACING COUNCIL SPECIAL REGULATIONS

For cruising and racing sailors, no small text contains more considered thought on what is safe and proper aboard an oceangoing sailboat than the slim 22-page document called *Special Regulations Governing Offshore Racing.*

Cruising sailors should not immediately see a red flag and mutter to themselves, "This is not for me." The rules written for offshore racers, as they appear, are superb guidelines for any sailboat being prepared to go to sea, whether a racing vessel or not. In many cases, the ORC regulations far exceed the minimum standards set by the Coast Guard or by the COLREGS. That is because the authors of the ORC regulations are responding to the very special activity of taking a small sailing vessel—one that is under 75 feet—out into the open and sometimes tempestuous waters of the sea. Experience has taught the offshore sailors who have contributed to the text many a hard lesson during thousands and thousands of miles of offshore sailing. The contributors have faced difficult situations, met and most often solved problems and given considerable thought to how to make the experience of sailing offshore safer and more fun.

The rules are written as guidelines for offshore race organizers and participants. They are written in shorthand and deal extensively with both racing and sailing protocol as well as the standards of safety and equipment required during an organized event. Events are divided into five categories: (0) transoceanic events; (1) offshore events; (2) extended races held along a shore; (3) races across open but protected waters (smaller lakes, bays); (4) short coastal races in protected waters.

While each category is treated throughout the ORC regulations, the aspects of the regulations that should be of paramount interest to offshore cruising and racing sailors are those which fall under Categories 0 and 1. The regulations of concern to most sailors are contained in six sections of the pamphlet, which we will cover below.

Structural Features

The intent of the rules governing the structural features of an offshore sailing boat is to provide the skipper of the boat with strict guidelines designed to keep water out of the boat. It's a simple and fundamental idea.

Boats built after 1986 must be built in accordance with the American Bureau of Shipping *Guide for Building Offshore and Racing*

Yachts. As a basic element of this requirement, no standing or running rigging may compromise the watertight integrity of the hull, deck or coach roof.

Hatches are always a concern when blue water is coming aboard in rough weather. Naturally, hatches must be built strongly. The rules also specify that they must not open into the boat if forward of the boat's maximum beam. And deck hatches must be placed so they are out of the water if the boat is knocked down to 90 degrees—a horizontal position. The companionway hatch must be able to be securely closed both from below and from on deck, while the hatch boards or hatch door must be able to be secured in place—against the possibility of a rollover—by a strong lanyard or a positive latch (deadbolt). Should a boat be rolled and inverted, even if only for a few seconds, the companionway hatches must not fall away leaving a massive, gaping leak in the boat.

The rules offer formulas for the permitted size of the cockpit well. Most, if not all, offshore sailing boats will comply. Of paramount concern, however, is the need for all hatches in the cockpit to be watertight and positively latched closed in bad weather. Experiencing a flood of water through an open cockpit locker is a thrill most sailors would sooner miss. Moreover, a cockpit must drain quickly and efficiently. Boats over 28 feet and built after 1972 must have at least two drains that measure no less than one inch each. The drains must also be covered by appropriate screens to prevent blockage.

Some modern boats have large saloon windows. Should these boats be readied for offshore sailing in an event governed by the ORC regulations, each window containing more than two square feet of opening must be fitted with a sturdy storm covering. Storm coverings should be fabricated of a sturdy material, such as Plexiglas, and should be fastened in place with sturdy, positive set screws or deadbolts.

All through-hulls must be fitted with appropriate sea cocks, with the exception of fittings for a depth sounder or speedo-log. All through-hulls must be equipped with soft wood plugs, which should be tied or wired into place adjacent to the sea cock or through-hull it services.

Vessels entered in Category 0—transoceanic—events are required to have one watertight bulkhead. This rule takes one line in the slim ORC booklet. Yet for skippers with boats that have been designed and built without such a bulkhead, this single line of text will cause the greatest expense and trouble; as he prepares to go to sea, however, it will also provide the ultimate in safety. It should be remembered that many boats have crossed oceans without a watertight bulkhead. It should also be remembered that every year more steel containers are jettisoned from the decks of ships, more flotsam litters the seas, and more submarines cruise at surface depth. If you are sailing in a Category 0 event, then compliance will not, in most cases, be optional. If you will be cruising offshore and making transoceanic runs, the decision to install a watertight bulkhead will have to be weighed carefully.

Lifelines on vessels over 28 feet must have two sets of lines and must be at least 24 inches off the deck. All pulpits and stanchions must be securely attached and the lines must have a tightening device to maintain the tautness of the wire.

Jackstays, which should be fitted on deck and in the cockpit on some boats, must be fitted in such a way that crew members can latch on with their safety harnesses before coming through the companionway, and can then latch onto the deck jackline to go forward before leaving the protection of the cockpit. The value of jacklines, for a crew busily moving fore and aft changing and reefing sails, will become apparent very quickly. Moving a latch from single point to single point is time-consuming and basically unsafe, for it exposes the sailor during the switch, and because the hassles tend to keep crew from wearing their harnesses in the first place. Being able to range fore and aft, attend to chores and set things right on the foredeck while holding on with one hand all the time as the harness shackle slides merrily along the jackline gives the sailor more peace of mind and a safer position on deck.

Accommodations

The rules governing the accommodations below decks are short and to the point. All furniture, tanks and galley equipment must be securely fastened in place. Should the boat roll to 90 degrees or farther, the interior of the boat should not be able to spring loose to injure those who are below.

Of particular concern is the galley stove, which may become the heaviest and most dangerous projectile in the cabin should it come loose. The regulations stipulate that the galley stove be secured against a full capsize and that the fuel line leading to the stove have a shutoff control that can be operated safely in a rough seaway.

General Equipment

The requirements for general onboard equipment call for the skipper to follow basic Coast Guard requirements and exercise some common sense. The skipper being addressed in this section is the skipper who might strip his boat of essential gear to lighten it for a racing speed advantage. The ORC frowns on this practice.

A special point is made in the regulations of the need for adequate bilge pumps. The rules state that a boat sailing in Category 0 or 1 events must have two manually operated bilge pumps with adequate hosing. One pump must be on deck while the other must be below. The second must be plumbed in such a way that it can be operated while all hatches are closed. Bilge pump handles must be permanently fitted into the bilge pump, or each pump handle must be provided with a lanyard or some other device to prevent its accidental loss. As a backup, two large 2-gallon buckets must also be carried.

The regulations specify that a boat over 28 feet must carry two anchors and appropriate rode and chain. These must be carried in such a way that they can be deployed quickly and efficiently. Boats under 28 feet must carry at least one anchor and tackle.

The regulations specify that all boats sailing in any of the categories be equipped with a radar reflector. The rule requires the reflector, if of the octahedral style, to have a minimum diagonal measurement of 18 inches. In other words, it must be large enough to register on a standard radar screen. If the reflector is of another type it must have a documented reflecting surface of not less than 10 square meters.

All boats must carry a set of international code flags. In addition, the boat must carry a guide to using the code flags so the crew can send a coded flag signal, even if the skipper is out of commission.

Lastly, fuel tanks on board must all have positive shutoff valves.

The requirements for general equipment set rigorous standards, yet they leave the prudent skipper with a list of only the most essential items that should appear on his list. Redundancy, in both gear and systems, is often the key to safe sailing. While the regulations call for redundancy in bilge pumps, buckets and elsewhere, the prudent skipper will equip himself, his crew and his boat with enough general gear and spares to provide for any mischance he may meet along his route.

Navigation Equipment

The rules mandate that a boat carry compasses, charts, lights lists and the appropriate navigational equipment. These items fall under the category of common sense.

Yet the rules also require the modern offshore sailing yacht to carry a sextant, sight-reduction tables and an accurate timepiece. In the day of loran, SatNav, GPS and all the other electronic aids to navigation, the sextant has become something of a relic. The ORC has taken the stand that no seaman should go to sea without the appropriate and traditional offshore navigation kit. While this is again common sense, every skipper should be reminded that a sextant will get him home, even when the lights and electronics aboard go out.

Among the navigational devices mandated by the rules is a radio direction finder (RDF) or some other automatic position-indicating device. This rule includes all the electronics one might wish to have aboard, yet the RDF is the most basic.

For the purposes of coastal navigation, the rules dictate that the boat be equipped with a depth sounder or lead line—most skippers carry both—as well as a speedometer and a log counter. All three are welcome aids should you find yourself making a landfall at night or in poor visibility.

Navigation lights are required by the COLREGS and by the Coast Guard. The ORC takes the requirement one step further by mandating that a backup system of navigation lights be aboard. The best installation of a backup system will be a redundant electrical installation. For example, a masthead tricolor can replace the deck-level running lights. However, should the electrical system on board fail, it is wise to also carry battery-operated navigation lights, which can be fixed to the rigging in an emergency.

Emergency Equipment

Fully half of the regulations covering emergency equipment involve sails and running rigging. The reason for this is simply that in a sailing vessel, the first responsibility of the skipper is to sail his vessel safely in all conditions and to bring her back to port no matter what conditions were met along the way.

To ensure that boats involved in Category 0 and 1 events are properly prepared to meet inclement weather and high winds, the ORC has set guidelines that provide for storm sailing. Boats must carry a storm trisail that can be flown independently of the mainsail's rigging and boom. The sail should be built of a cloth heavy enough to withstand high winds. Every boat must carry a storm jib, which must have its own rigging and must be strong enough to hold up in high winds. And every boat must carry a heavy weather jib—a number three or four—which is heavy enough to stand up to strong winds and cut to drive the boat to windward. The heavy weather jib must not contain reef points, nor may it be a larger sail reefed down to a smaller size.

On boats with roller-furling headstays, there must be a secondary method for flying the heavy weather jib from the headstay. While roller-furling systems have proven themselves reliable over millions of miles of offshore sailing, it is only prudent to plan for the rare occasion when the roller system fails.

Emergency steering is key to offshore preparedness. Under the regulations, every boat must be provided with an emergency tiller that is fitted to the rudder stock. Such equipment is standard aboard almost every sailing vessel, but it is required when sailing in an ORC event. Additionally, the crew of every boat should be aware of alternate methods of steering the boat—with warps, buckets, sails and so on—in the event that the rudder itself fails. The rules stipulate that, prior to an ORC event, an inspector may ask a crew to demonstrate how such emergency steering will be accomplished.

A complete tool kit should be on board for mending standing and running rigging and other sailing systems. In addition, a boat must be equipped with a device, such as a heavy-duty bolt cutter, with which to sever the standing rig from the hull should the mast come down and, lying alongside, threaten to punch a hole in the hull.

Every boat must carry a marine transmitter and receiver. Most skippers will opt for a standard marine VHF radio. If so, that radio must be equipped not only with its primary antenna at the masthead, but also with an emergency antenna, which can be deployed should the masthead antenna be lost or should the mast itself come down.

Additionally, every boat must carry a radio that is capable of receiving weather forecasts and bulletins. The best choice is a high-seas multi-band receiver, with an appropriate antenna.

For emergency signaling via radio, the rules specify that you must carry an emergency position-indicating radio beacon (EPIRB) that will broadcast a distress signal on Channels 121.5, 243 or 406 MHz.

Lastly, the regulations stipulate that at least two gallons of water per crew member be carried for emergency use. This emergency water supply can be carried in one or more separate containers.

Safety Equipment

Safety equipment differs from emergency equipment in the degree of emergency addressed. While the regulations on emergency equipment cover sailing situations, high winds and communications, safety equipment is aimed at the next level of danger.

The rules specify that a life preserver be carried for each crew member. Yet unlike the Coast Guard, the ORC has chosen to set the minimum buoyancy for those life jackets at 16 kilograms or 35 pounds of buoyancy. Moreover, the jackets must be designed to hold an unconscious person upright at an angle of 45 degrees while in the water. Each life jacket must be fitted with a whistle and should be marked with reflective tape.

Safety harnesses must be carried for each member of the crew. While the regulations are brief on the subject of safety harnesses, the entirety of Appendix I is devoted to the subject. No other item of gear specified by the regulations has been given as much scrutiny as the life harness. The reason is obvious. The greatest danger at sea is losing a person overboard. The single best way to keep a person on board is to equip that person with an appropriate—strong, well designed, well built—harness.

Every boat must carry a life raft that can hold the entire crew. The raft must be readily available to the crew—it must be able to be launched within 15 seconds—and must have a valid inspection certificate on the canister or valise. In most instances, the best installation will be on deck. Yet if a raft is to be stored below decks, it may not weigh more than 40 kilograms or 90 pounds and must be capable of being launched within the 15-second minimum.

To deal with a man-overboard emergency, the boat must be equipped with a life buoy with a drogue, or a Lifesling. The life buoy must be fitted with a self-igniting light and must be positioned near the helmsman. In addition to the first life buoy, a second is required, which is attached to a marking pole—dan buoy—that is at least six feet high and equipped with a flag at its top. The life buoy should have a whistle and a dye marker attached, as well as a self-igniting light.

In 1989 the ORC ruled that it is acceptable to carry a full man-overboard rig—buoy, pole, light, dye and whistle—and supplement that with a commercial Lifesling instead of a second buoy. For many sailors, this combination will be the sensible choice.

Visual distress signals are required, but unlike the COLREGS or the Coast Guard, the ORC mandates that boats carry SOLAS-grade flares. The following are required for Category 0 and 1 and must be stored in a watertight container:

12 red parachute flares
 4 red hand-held flares
 4 white hand-held flares
 2 orange smoke day signals

Flares that are more than three years old, as dated by the manufacturer, will not be accepted by event organizers using the ORC regulations.

Lastly, every boat is required to have a 50-foot heaving line close to the helmsman that can be tossed quickly, accurately and to a reasonable distance to a man in the water.

THE ORC REGULATIONS are the highest standards set in the world of offshore and coastal sailing. For the novice, the Coast Guard regulations are a legal requirement. They are also a good place to start in the process of deciding what you need to carry aboard your boat for the safety of your boat and its crew.

For those who have set their sights on coastal and offshore sailing—particularly those who own boats of 39 feet or more—the COLREGS are the next step in preparation and equipment. The COLREGS, which embody the rules of the road and the international standards of protocol and seamanship, should be considered a base of knowledge all the members of the crew should strive for.

And if you are headed offshore or on long coastal trips that take you out of the usual paths of coastal sailing, then the ORC special regulations offer an excellent guide to safety, emergency preparedness and much more.

The safe skipper will study all three sources of information and regulations from the pros and will take to heart the vast experience and sea time that have gone into the formulation and writing of the rules and standards. The pros have been out there and have come back to help us all sail more safely on the high seas.

Chapter 4

SAFE DECKS AND SAFE BELOW

Foredeck, Side Decks and the Cockpit
A Safe Saloon and Galley

IN SOME OF the great voyaging ports of the world you will find cruising boats that have sailed many thousands of miles. Along the way, these boats' skippers have refined their vessels, adding and eliminating gear, to the point where they have created efficient and safe ocean-sailing boats. The first time I encountered this type of vessel was in the Canary Islands, many years ago. The boats gathered in Las Palmas—most of which flew European flags—were girded for the transatlantic push to the Caribbean. As these craft swung on their anchors in the oily harbor in front of the Yacht Club de Grand Canaria, they each had an aura of seaworthiness and experience—even though most had only voyaged a few thousand miles or less.

This same impression can be found in the boats at anchor in ports such as Balboa, Panama; or Papeete, Tahiti; or the Bay of Islands, New Zealand. Here you find boats that are tried and true, sailed by

The offshore cruising ketch *Dione*, owned by veteran voyagers Brian and Judy Harrison, is an excellent example of a heavily built, thoughtfully designed passagemaker. *Dione* has cruised around the world and sailed some 100,000 miles.

skippers who have tested their initial ideas of what should be aboard a cruising boat against the real experience of sailing far and wide.

In most cases, the boats you find moored in such places have a businesslike look. Their decks may be somewhat laden with gear, but the on-deck systems are simple, efficient and arranged for easy and safe handling in bad conditions.

Equally important, down below on these boats you will find cozy floating homes that are fitted out not for life at a marina, but for life at sea. Everything has a place from which it cannot fall. All hatches have positive latches and all heavy accoutrements—from batteries to the galley stove—are well secured.

Moreover, both on deck and down below, you will find handholds everywhere on these bluewater boats. Skippers who have spent a few thousand miles or more on the open sea know that the old adage, "One hand for the ship and one for yourself," is as true today as the day it was uttered.

In the preceding chapters we have discussed the preparations a skipper makes in order to arrive safely from a passage out on the open sea; we have taken a look at yacht design and what makes for a safe sailing vessel; and we have discussed the safety rules, codes and regulations written by sailors with millions of miles of experience behind them.

It is time, here, to take a good look at how these ideas can be put into practice in the layout and fitting out of safe deck arrangements, both above and below.

Every skipper when he sets out to sea, whether along a coast or across an ocean, has two primary objectives regarding safe deck and down-below layouts: First, the crew must be able to stay on board; and, second, gear and objects below must never be lethal flying hazards, no matter how far the boat rolls to a gust of wind.

For some veteran sailors, the need to secure the furniture and objects below and to arrange the deck to make sure everyone stays on board is made evident after the first heavy weather passage. However, experience has taught most sailors to prepare for difficulties before setting out and to provide systems that will ensure the two main seafaring objectives.

FOREDECK, SIDE DECKS AND THE COCKPIT

Every sailing boat will have its own deck arrangement, so the need to apply the basic guidelines for safe decks will vary from design to design. Yet there are simple and basic practices to follow on any boat that will keep the crew prepared for whatever may come. The illustration shown below gives a general layout of what should be installed and provided on deck and how it should work together.

Our discussion begins at the foredeck. It is important for crew members working forward of the mast to be able to work headsails, lines and gear while attached by their safety harnesses to stout and readily available fittings and jacklines. It is useful to tie stops through the toerail or stanchion bases on either side of the foredeck

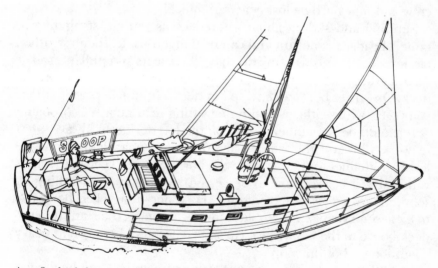

A safe deck layout will be uncluttered and well thought out for the well-being of the crew. The foredeck and side decks should have jacklines. All halyards and sheets should have secure places once coiled. The main sheet and boom should not be a hazard. Items stowed on deck—dinghy, life raft, sails, sailboard—should be securely tied down.

so a crew member always has a quick length of line or sail tie with which to tie down a sail or other gear that might come loose.

Many offshore sailors and those who cruise with children use netting, which is commercially available, in their lifelines on either side of the foredeck. The netting, reaved of nylon line, will prevent a small person from falling overboard, catch a headsail that has come adrift during a sail change and help to keep loose items such as sail bags, docking lines and other equipment on board. The netting should be stretched firmly into place and secured at the top and along the bottom with a strong piece of line. If possible, it is best to weave the top course of the netting right onto the lifeline. To do this you will have to unmake the lifelines and remake them again with the netting attached. Despite the trouble, this arrangement is both the safest and the neatest looking.

Foredeck gear, such as anchor tackle, line, spare headsails, spinnaker poles, even a life raft, should be securely fastened to the deck, either with sail ties or with strong line. Loose gear is a hazard to the crew and may become lost gear very quickly.

Slipping and sliding about a foredeck as you are struggling to tame a headsail is no fun and can be dangerous. In rough weather, old foredeck hands will sink down on their seats and pull in a sail or manhandle loose gear while well planted by the rear end on the deck. On larger boats with wide foredecks, finding a place to brace your feet, while either standing or sitting, can be a real problem.

It should be remembered that on the foredeck, it is always safest to work while on the windward side of the boat, away from the leeward lifelines and away from the bow wake. To keep yourself to windward, it is necessary to brace your feet against something. A solution favored years ago on some classic one-design keel boats was to fix a wood strip, approximately an inch square, that ran from the deck house to the bow. The strip served as a foot brace or, in heavy conditions, a bottom stop.

Installing such a strip—or two strips off center—can be a good solution on wide-form modern cruising boats. However, before installing such a strip, you should consider the hazard it will present to bare toes, to sunbathers and to those in the crew who tend to hurry about on deck.

Working around the mast, a crew member should feel secure and have the ability to use both hands to operate a winch while raising a halyard or coiling lines. It is important that sturdy padeyes be fitted, either on deck or near the base of the mast, onto which safety harnesses can be clipped. These padeyes should be situated in such a way as to keep the harness tether out of the way of working halyards and sheets.

On larger boats, there will be room enough around the mast on the cabin top to install stainless steel braces or "sissy bars." The derogatory nickname stems from the bars of the same name found on some old-style motorcycles. On the cycles, the bars prevent a rider from being seriously injured should the machine tip over in a slide. On deck, the bars will serve a similar function by offering a crew member a place to brace himself while working at the mast. The sissy bars should be of sturdy stainless steel, through-bolted and backed with aluminum backing plates. They can also serve as places to tie down spare sails, to store spare sail ties and to fasten flag halyards that lead to the spreaders.

While we are discussing the foredeck and mainmast area, it may be worthwhile to mention deck boxes. Although it may be stretching the point to include boxes in a discussion of safety, proper deck boxes can, in fact, offer quick and easy storage places for tools and gear that may be needed in a hurry by the person on the foredeck.

It may be useful to picture a sudden need for an adjustable wrench and a screwdriver. Imagine the forestay suddenly sagging because the cotter pins in the turnbuckle have failed. The jib must come down quickly and should be tied down with the sail ties already in place along the toe rail. Next, the person on the foredeck must tighten and secure the headstay. The job will be accomplished more easily and quickly if the needed tools are at hand. Having to burrow into a locker below and then dash back to the foredeck will delay the repair and could make it impossible. A deck box, no matter how large or small, equipped with a few essential tools, docking lines, sail ties and winch handles, will make life on the foredeck safer and easier.

For coastal cruising most skippers do not choose to carry heavy weather and storm sails on deck. Yet, those setting off across wide bodies of water in areas in which a gale might be encountered will want to rig storm sails for ready use. The most common setup on offshore boats is to carry a storm trisail to be flown on the main-mast. The trisail should have its own sail track on the mast, running parallel to the mainsail's track or slot. The sail itself can be bagged tightly and stowed on deck at the base of the mast, or it can be stowed below. The storm jib or spitfire jib can usually be stowed below. Yet, if bad weather is imminent, the sails should be brought on deck and rigged in place—before they become necessary—to avoid painstaking foredeck and mast work when the going gets rough. The trisail track and spitfire setup should be in place at all times for those who carry such gear. There is no use carrying emergency sails and running rigging if you are not prepared to use them when the wind and seas kick up.

Moving aft, the side decks leading from the cockpit to the fore-deck are the hallways to and from the mast and foredeck. As pre-scribed in the ORC regulations and as dictated by common sense, the side decks should be fitted with jacklines that run from the cockpit coaming to the bow. It should be possible for a person to clip a harness tether onto the jacklines while still in the cockpit and then move all the way forward and back again without having to unclip to change anchor points.

The standard jackline is a length of 1-by-19 wire, coated with plastic and swaged at its ends. The ends are then attached to heavy padeyes that are through-bolted and backed with aluminum plates. One hazard presented by jacklines arises because the round wire, if rigged loosely on deck, can roll underfoot, causing a person to lose his balance. For that reason, some sailors prefer to rig jacklines made of woven webbing of the type used in safety harnesses. This webbing is extremely strong, absorbs strain and lies flat on the deck. However, webbing deteriorates in sunlight and must be checked often for strength.

For jacklines to be effective, the crew must be able to attach to the lines before leaving the companionway and entering the cockpit, and then must be able to switch into the deck jacklines before leaving the cockpit for the foredeck. The best arrangements call for either a number of sturdy padeyes both at the companionway and next to the helmsman's seat, or two jacklines running the length of the cockpit on either side of the cockpit foot well.

While using harnesses and jacklines once the rig has been installed properly would seem to fall under the umbrella of common sense, it is wise to remember that the crew should use the windward rather than leeward attachments. The reason is simply gravity. If you fall from the windward side to leeward, the windward attachment may break your fall and will keep you close to the boat should you go over the side. If you are attached to leeward, your fall will occur unbroken and should you fall overboard, you will stream out to the full length of your tether, putting enormous strain on the jacklines, fittings and harness—not to mention yourself.

Hatches on deck are the largest openings into the boat and should be treated with respect and a certain amount of suspicion. Most modern deck hatches are fabricated of extruded aluminum and have Plexiglas or Lexan securely bedded in the openings; most have thick, durable weather seals and positive dogging devices to keep them closed. However, as a matter of course before setting out for any length of time on the water, every hatch should be checked thoroughly and the dogging devices—hand screws or friction levers—made as tight as possible.

On boats with large wood hatches or decorative skylights, it is wise to have canvas (or Sunbrella) covers ready to fit over the hatch when bad weather hits. Although a cloth cover, no matter how securely tied over a hatch, will not prevent the whole hatch from being carried away by a malicious wave, it will prevent minor damage and will keep water out of the boat should the wood frame of the hatch become cracked or damaged.

The Cockpit

On most cruising boats the cockpit is the place where the crew spends the majority of its time, whether under sail or at anchor. The cockpit must fulfill many functions: It is command central while the boat is sailing; it is the place where most deck gear, sheets, lines and sailing equipment is kept; it serves as a patio for topsides meals and cocktails and it is the place where most safety and emergency gear is kept. Without doubt, the cockpit requires more organization than any other area of the boat.

One of the best ways to keep your crew happy and functioning at a safe level is to make sure everyone is warm and dry. Appropriate

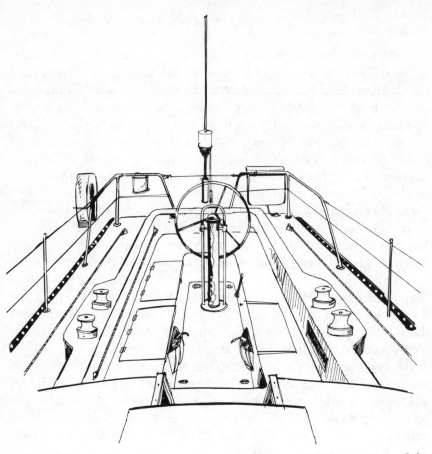

Arrange the cockpit so it is well organized, lines and sheets are out of the way, there are plenty of handholds and the crew can be protected from wind, spray and weather.

clothing is the first step. But rigging the cockpit with a doghouse, dodger or weather cloths will make a large difference.

A dodger of some sort is a necessary addition to any sailing boat heading off shore. The dodger should be sturdily built, with stainless-steel tubing used in the frame. The frame must be able to withstand the weight of a man falling against it or the weight of the boom should it fall a short distance. The frame should be securely fastened to the deck and to the sea hood that covers the companionway hatch. Although the frame-and-fabric dodger conventionally seen on cruising boats will not hold up to the force of a breaking wave on deck, it should be expected to withstand high winds and rain and the normal wear and tear of years of sailing. It is important to have heavy plastic windows sewn into the side and front of the dodger to provide for forward visibility. And, the fabric selected should be waterproof, have resistance to ultraviolet deterioration and have very little elasticity. Sunbrella is often used, but other waterproofed fabrics are also suitable.

Weather cloths that can be tied securely against the lifelines on either side of the cockpit will protect the helmsman and crew from the wind and spray coming over the side. On a blustery day, it is quite a relief for those in the cockpit to get out of the wind. Moreover, providing a wind-and-spray break will help those in the cockpit stay warm, thereby inhibiting the possibilities of hypothermia. The weather cloths should be made of sturdy material—Dacron or Sunbrella—and have reinforced patches under the grommets. The cloths should run from the last stanchion or the stern pulpit to the stanchion forward of the cockpit. On most boats you will have to provide cutouts through which jib sheets may pass. And, if you plan to use the weather cloths often, it is useful to have two or three storage pockets sewn onto the inside of the cloths.

Providing for smooth sail handling with a well-thought-out cockpit will lessen confusion during sailing maneuvers and help to prevent accidents or mishaps. When organizing sailing gear and lines, make sure that everything has a place and is always kept there. Winch handles should be tucked into holders in the corners of the cockpit, and it is best to have one handle for each side of the boat. During a tack, no one should be hunting around for the lone handle that somehow is missing.

Headsail sheets and the main sheet are usually under a lot of strain. Too often the sheets are left to collect in piles in the cockpit where feet can become entangled and the sheets themselves can become a braided mess. To clear the decks, a simple and good solution is to provide bags fastened to the inside of the cockpit foot well into which coiled sheets can be tucked out of the way. Since the main sheet may be too large and too long to package this way, you may want to designate a specific area where the main sheet can be flaked out of the crew's way.

In the past few years, the practice of leading halyards aft from the mainmast to the cockpit has come into favor. Doing so can keep crew safely in the cockpit during sail changes. On boats with roller-furling headsails and a roller-furling main, there is no longer any reason to leave the cockpit while handling sails.

The drawback to leading everything aft to the cockpit is simply that one person can no longer operate halyards while also dropping headsails or tying in a reef. If a person has to go forward, then a second will have to man the halyards from the cockpit. Also, leading halyards through a series of turning blocks adds friction to the sail-hoisting process and may require that you use a larger winch.

These caveats mentioned, it is still a wise move to lead halyards aft. With a little ingenuity and the use of some of the single-line sail-handling systems now on the market, sail handling from the cockpit can be both efficient and safe.

The main boom may be the most dangerous piece of gear on the boat. It is a head cracker that can, in a second, fling a person, unconscious, over the side. To tame the boom, it is wise to use both a preventer guy and a vang. The preventer guy, which on cruising boats can be left rigged at all times, runs from the aft end of the boom through a block or fitting on the foredeck. On a broad reach or a dead run, the boom can be fixed in place by the preventer so a sudden jibe won't send the boom careening across the deck.

A vang, which is used primarily to shape the mainsail, will also control the vertical movement of the boom and keep it from jumping unexpectedly. A hydraulic vang, or Quick-vang, which is fixed between the boom and the base of the mast, will hold the boom stationary while you reef or drop the sail. Such a vang cannot be rigged to leeward to double as preventer. A three-part vang-tackle is a useful addition, for you can use it in a number of ways, including using it as a preventer from the middle of the boom to the leeward rail. Rigged in such a way, the tackle will inhibit flying jibes, while simultaneously flattening the mainsail.

A third option is the use of the Walder Boom-brake. The brake attaches to the center of the boom and permits the boom to move slowly and steadily across the boat during a tack or controlled jibe. However, in a flying jibe, the brake will catch the boom, preventing it from lifting and swinging dangerously across the boat. The Walder

The mast and foredeck layout on the Navy 44 is a good example of a safe, thoughtful layout. Note the "sissy bars" over the Dorade vents, the nonskid surface on the forehatches, the halyard winches mounted on deck where the crew can work sitting down and the secure mast boot to keep water from migrating below decks.

Boom-brake was made popular in the United States in the mid-1980s, following the first BOC Challenge, a single-handed around-the-world race. Philippe Jeantot won the race and used the Walder Boom-brake all the way around the world.

The helmsman's position in the cockpit, most often behind the binnacle and wheel, should be arranged so the helmsman can reach vital gear while still keeping one hand on the wheel. It is customary to keep a knife, a pair of binoculars, and perhaps a small hand-bearing compass near the helmsman's seat.

In addition, most modern boats are built with a high-volume manual bilge pump located under or near the helmsman's seat, where it can be operated while the boat is being steered. It is necessary to arrange a place near the pump for the handle, where the helmsman can reach it quickly yet where it also can be stowed securely out of the way. You don't want to find yourself needing the pump but being unable to use it because the essential handle has disappeared. One simple way to secure the handle near the pump is to sew a small pouch for it with a Velcro closure at the top that can be fastened directly to the sidewall of the foot well.

Safety gear and man-overboard equipment most often will be arranged aft of the helmsman on the stern pulpit or on the stern deck. In a man-overboard emergency, the ability to deploy gear quickly and easily can make the difference between a scare and a disaster.

Standard equipment that should be rigged on the aft pulpit includes: a throwable horseshoe ring and life ring, equipped with a dan buoy, an automatic strobe and a whistle; a second throwable horseshoe or a Lifesling; and a coiled heaving line. The horseshoe, pole and light should be arranged so all the helmsman has to do is toss the ring into the water and the rest of the gear will follow. The pole, which is usually mounted on the backstay or on a mizzen sidestay, should be able to break from its fastenings easily and quickly.

A boat sailing at six knots is moving through the water and away from a man overboard at approximately 10 feet per second. Even a strong swimmer can not be expected to swim very far after falling overboard, particularly if he is fully clothed or was injured in some way during the fall. Therefore, it is essential that the man-overboard pole and horseshoe be set up for deployment in less than five seconds.

The heaving line, which should be at least 50 feet long and have a Turk's Head or some other weight at its end, should be handy to the helmsman. There are several commercial lines available, fitted with a pouch and made from polypropylene line which floats. Although you can make up your own line, the commercial option offers you a useful tool at a low price.

The second horseshoe buoy or the Lifesling should be mounted on the stern rail opposite to the man-overboard rig. We will discuss the use of the Lifesling and all of the man-overboard equipment in Chapter 7. At this point, suffice it to say that the horseshoe or Lifesling should be easy to deploy and everyone on board should know how to use all the gear quickly and easily.

Safety on deck and in the cockpit requires planning and fore-thought. As you examine your own boat for ways to make the decks safer and the cockpit better organized, run through a wide range of sailing scenarios to make certain that the gear and systems you are adding will enhance safety while improving the working efficiency of the boat.

A SAFE SALOON AND GALLEY

In recent years, the builders of production boats for coastal and offshore sailing have been forced by consumers and marketing experts to serve two very different masters when laying out and building the interiors of their boats. On the vast majority of new boats the main saloons have been designed to be wide, open spaces that give one the feeling of airiness and opulence below. This interior design trend seeks to attract buyers. However, it does not necessarily serve the sailor's best interests.

If you have ever tried to exist below during a rough patch of sailing aboard a boat with a wide, open saloon, you will know that such a space can be a real hazard. On such a boat, with 12 or 13 feet of beam, one fall from the windward side can toss a person into a heap 10 feet or so to leeward.

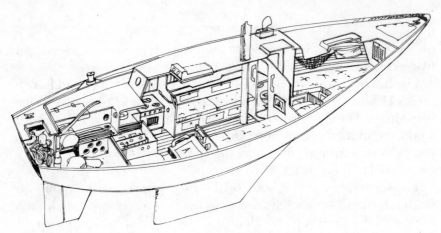

Down below, the cabin should be safe for all who are not working on deck. Handholds need to be strategically placed. Lockers must have positive latches or dead bolts. Floorboards should be well secured. Bunks should have sturdy weather cloths. And the galley should be arranged so it is possible to cook, safe from the threat of scalding or burns.

As on deck, the first and most important pieces of gear below decks are numerous and well-positioned handholds. The handholds should be at waist height—not solely overhead or running beneath the port holes—and should be positioned in such a way that a person can work his way all the way forward and aft while moving from one handhold to another.

On many modern boats, the saloon table is not designed to support the weight of a lurching body. The fittings for the table should be inspected and strengthened if necessary. If the boat is wide and the danger of flying across it is great, a simple solution is to install a stainless-steel pole from the floor to the deck head. The pole will offer a solid anchor for the crew and can become an additional brace for the saloon table.

Falling while moving about the boat can be dangerous. But falling out of a bunk while resting or sleeping during an offwatch, can be a real nuisance. Every berth that will be used for sleeping while sailing through the night should be equipped with a sturdy lee cloth. A lee cloth, usually sewn of canvas with grommets at the free corners, is fastened to the bunk frame under the cushion. When not in use, it folds away under the cushion. When in use, the lee cloth is rigged by tying the corners tightly to padeyes or handholds over the berth. The cloth should span the berth from the sleeper's shoulders to well below the hip, but it need not be the full length of the berth. Lastly, the weather cloth should be rigged in such a way that the last tie—at the head—can be made once the crew member is in the berth.

In a rough sea that has the boat bucking and leaping, it is not uncommon for books to jump off shelves, for locker doors to swing open disgorging their contents onto the floor and for other gear to migrate randomly around the cabin. There may be no greater danger to the crew in bad weather than to face heavy objects that have broken loose. The solution is to provide positive latches or deadbolts on any lid, door, drawer or floorboard that could come loose.

The most dangerous objects below are the stove and the batteries. A gimballed stove, weighing 50 or more pounds, can be a lethal flying object if it breaks loose from its gimbals. It is important to check the bolts and the fittings on the stove and oven to make certain that even in a knockdown, with the boat lying for a moment on its beam ends, the stove will remain securely in place. The batteries, which may be under a berth or below the floorboards, should be fixed in place with positive and sturdy fastenings. The best approach is to bolt restraining braces from the hull over the batteries. With the nuts tightened down, even a rollover won't send the batteries flying.

Floorboards, usually fabricated of marine plywood, can cause serious injuries should they come loose. There are several commercial latches available to secure floorboards in place, although such latches are too seldom used in production boats. Latched in place, the floorboards will remain tightly attached to the floor beams, even in a knockdown.

Ice box and freezer compartment lids are another source of possible injury during poor weather. The lids are often heavy, have sharp corners where Formica is joined at the edges and too often rely on gravity to keep them in place. In a knockdown or rollover, the lids can and will come loose. The best way to secure ice box lids is to fit them with dead bolts. Yet the bolts will be a constant nuisance for those working in the galley. Another approach is to fix the lids in place with stainless steel piano hinges. While a piano hinge is not a positive latch, it will inhibit the lids from unplanned flights across the cabin and can be installed flush with the countertop.

Working in the galley while sailing on the wind can be a devilish problem. As the boat bucks into the wind and heels to gusts, food on the stove, items being prepared on the counter and the cook himself will be knocked around. The danger of being scalded from a pot of simmering spaghetti sauce is very real. It is important that the stove top be fitted with stainless steel fiddles or pot holders that can clamp a sauce pan in place.

There is some controversy among sailors about the use of galley belts, which can be hooked across the galley to provide the cook with a seat or, on the opposite tack, a belt to lean against. The belt will hold you in place while you are trying to wrest a meal from the galley. However, once strapped in with the belt, there is no way for the cook to leap out of the way of dangerous airborne spaghetti sauce.

On a boat that has a securely gimballed stove and stove top fitted with fiddles to hold pots in place, the galley belt should be more of a

Cruising World/George Day

The main saloon of the Navy 44 a simple layout with good sea berths, simple tackle arrangements for leecloths, plenty of handholds and an airy, open plan that will not induce seasickness among those off watch.

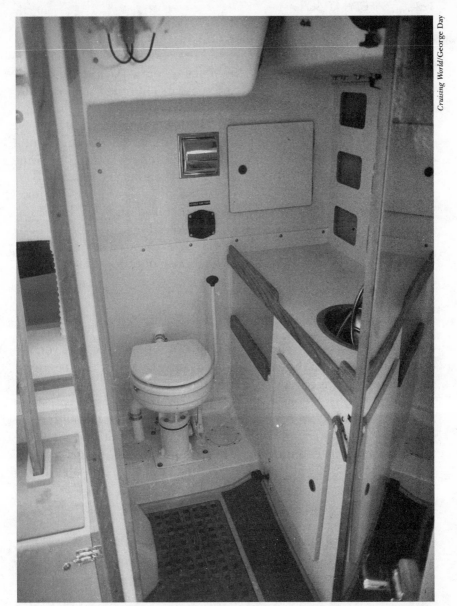

Cruising World/George Day

The head is often ignored as a design feature. Yet arranging the head properly is a must on an oceangoing vessel. The fore and aft placement of the head on the Navy 44, positioned in the center of the boat, means that users will not be thrown off the throne when the boat rolls and that the motion in the head from pitching and rolling will be at a minimum.

benefit than a danger. However, to ensure that hot soups and sauces stay where they belong, experienced sea cooks make a practice of never filling sauce pans above the halfway mark. Keeping the pot's center of gravity low will greatly increase its tendency to stay on the stove.

Safety equipment below should be positioned where it will be readily available. If you need a fire extinguisher, you will need it in a hurry, so make sure the extinguishers required by law and by common sense are placed within easy reach. If you carry an EPIRB, it should be mounted near the companionway for quick retrieval should you need it. Safety harnesses, which too often get buried at the bottom of the wet locker, should be stowed near the companionway where they will be ready at hand. If the harnesses are not convenient to the crew, the crew will choose not to wear them.

SETTING UP YOUR boat for safe sailing will take a lot of thought and preparation. On deck you will have to anticipate how you will handle sails and gear in a wide range of situations. The way you lay out deck gear can make the difference between a boat that is safe to sail and one that is an accident waiting to happen.

Similarly, down below, if the real problems of trying to eat, sleep and navigate while under way have not been thought through thoroughly, a simple overnight sail can turn into a chaotic and unpleasant experience. A cabin that is secure, a galley that is pleasant and safe to work in and bunks that are comfortable and cozy all add up to safe and pleasant sailing.

Chapter 5

DRESS FOR SUCCESS AND SAFETY

Staying on Board
Protection from the Weather
Survival Gear
The Sailor's Kit

THE SIGHT OF a high-tech racing machine cutting through the waves hard on the wind, tossing a bow wave and leaving a foaming wake astern, is awe-inspiring. The sails are trimmed to perfection, the sheets and halyards are tucked away in their places—bagged or coiled—and the afterguard is intently studying the boat's progress as the helmsman steers to the groove.

And on the rail, six or eight or ten crewmen, in matching white foul weather gear bearing the boat's insignia, lean to the wind.

To many sailors, this picture conjures up the very best in sailing. It evokes speed, it spells seamanship and experience, and it virtually hollers state of the art.

Perhaps it is.

But there is one thing wrong with this picture. On the rail, the

A warm, dry crew will be a happy crew.

able crew has been fitted out with foul weather gear that will keep the wearers dry but has been designed to suit fashion more than the needs of the sea. White foul weather gear, which looks stunning in magazine photographs or tossed over the back of a yacht club chair, is the last thing you would want to wear should you ever need to be seen—should you ever be in the water on a dark night waving to a crew that is desperately trying to find you.

Aboard a boat that is sailing any distance, along the coast or offshore, the clothes you wear must first conform to function and only secondarily conform to the fashion of the day.

If you have ever lost overboard a white deck cushion or a white sun hat and gone back to retrieve it, you will know how difficult it is to see a white object against the blue and white or black and white hues of the sea. Those who have made a profession of lifesaving have developed colors that can be seen: international orange, bright yellow, luminous green and reflective silver. Selecting foul weather gear of another color—white or blue in particular—is only asking for trouble.

Clothing for sailors performs four general functions: staying on board; staying warm and dry; surviving in a worst-case situation; and safety and utility on deck. Making the right and prudent choice in the clothing you wear while sailing can be the difference between safety afloat and an unnecessary accident. Knowing the difference between what is fashionable and what is functional can be all-important.

STAYING ON BOARD

The popularity of rubber-soled moccasins fashioned after the original Topsider deck shoe has dressed a large percentage of the population in shoes that were once conceived to keep a sailor's feet on deck, dry and comfortable. The leather upper, rubber lower, corrugated sole deck shoe is now the standard in leisure wear. Possibly only blue jeans have reached a wider consuming audience.

But the old-style deck shoes' winning ways are not due to purpose of their design. The shoes are comfortable, they conform to a wide variety of feet and they seem almost ageless. So they are popular.

But the shoe style was designed to keep a sailor from skidding around dangerously on deck. The moccasin shoe was chosen for its durability and its ability to withstand repeated soaking, but the innovation in the shoe was the ribbed or corrugated sole. The sole, now imitated by dozens of manufacturers, is designed to gutter water away from the middle of the sole to the edges, leaving more-or-less dry rubber to meet the deck.

This simple idea may have saved thousands of lives, for the deck shoe gives the wearer double protection. As most sailors know, a bare foot may offer good traction on a wet deck. But at the end of bare feet there are bare toes, which have an uncanny way of stubbing themselves against immovable objects such as padeyes, anchors, chain plates and turning blocks. The deck shoe gives those toes protection and gives the wearer excellent traction.

Often overlooked, the simple deck shoe, no matter what fashion trend it may be following, may be the most important item of safety gear you and your crew can bring aboard your boat. Many skippers

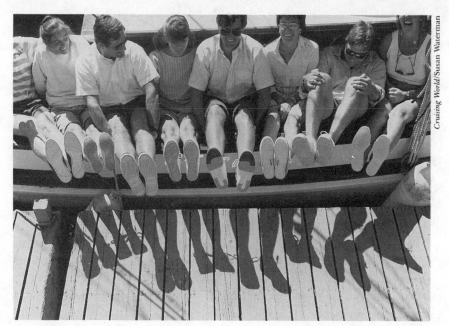

Top quality nonskid footwear is essential for all working on deck. Deck shoes should have soles that drain water away while they grip the deck. And the shoes should have solid toes to prevent stubs that could toss a crew member overboard.

who have watched their fellow sailors slip and slide, stub their toes and tumble precariously, require all on board to wear shoes whenever on deck.

Deck shoes now are sold as moccasins, or running shoe clones, as non-skid socks or as sea boots. The variety in moccasins offers everything from dress shoes to thick-soled woodsman's wear. The trick is to find a shoe that both suits your foot and suits the decks you'll be sailing on. While you may wear moccasins as casual shoes at any time, choose your boat shoes by their soles and for their purpose afloat. It is good to remember that softer soles grip better than harder soles and larger patterned gutters grip better than tighter patterns. Moccasins for sailing should be used only for sailing. Shoes for the yacht club can be chosen for their style.

The new styles of deck shoes patterned on running shoes have given sailors light, comfortable footwear that combines the technology of running shoes and the non-skid soles of sailing shoes. Most have serviceable soles that will keep you on your feet and most have uppers that dry quickly and keep their shape. The better shoes have removable insoles, which is a boon because the one hazard with the running-deck shoe is sneaker rot. After repeated drenchings, the running-type shoe that has not been completely dried will begin a biological life all its own, complete with the odors that go with such swamp decay. In general, the running shoe style wears better and gives a better grip than moccasins, but lasts about half as long.

The latest in nonskid shoes is the rubber-soled sock, called the Reef Runner by one company that markets it. These brightly colored items evolved from board sailing and provide excellent grip on the deck, fast-drying fabrics and tight fit. It is hard to imagine a crew of die-hard sailors in foul weather gear wearing nonskid socks but, of all the dedicated onboard footwear, these newcomers may be the best suited to keeping your feet comfortable and your body on the boat.

Sea boots should be part of every serious sailor's sea kit. On a long night watch or in cool weather, warm, dry feet will do more to maintain morale than 50 gallons of hot cocoa. Sea boots, like deck shoes, have evolved to the point where it is possible to own light, high boots that have excellent non-skid soles. Most sea boots come without inner liners. If you want to upgrade your boots, adding felt or polypropylene insoles can make a real difference. Choose your boots first by their soles and only then by the color of the rubber and the style of the drawstring.

While shoes may seem trivial when thinking about safety at sea, it is worth remembering that one, small sure step for a crewman on deck is worth all the man-overboard gear you may be carrying. Good, nonskid shoes are the first line of defense against a mishap.

STAYING ON BOARD is every individual crew member's responsibility. Wearing a safety harness should be required when sailing at night or in bad weather. However, no matter what the weather, it is prudent to carry a harness for everyone on board.

Harnesses occupy such an important place in the pantheon of safety gear that the Offshore Racing Council (ORC) devotes fully a quarter of its pamphlet *Special Regulations Governing Offshore Racing* to them. The standards set out by the ORC call for harnesses to be constructed of heavy, synthetic webbing, with a belt and braces. The buckle should fit the wearer so that the tether is located at armpit level. The tether itself should be no longer than six feet and the hooks must be self-latching and capable of withstanding a load of 1,500 pounds.

It is important, when looking for harnesses for the crew, to purchase those that are simple to put on, comfortable to wear and adjustable enough to fit over either a T-shirt or heavy foul weather gear.

There are several good brands on the market, but those made by Steve Lirakis of Newport, Rhode Island, are considered by many offshore sailors to be the best. The Lirakis harness is robustly made, heavily sewn and fitted with hooks that exceed the ORC recommendations. Although somewhat more expensive than other brands, the Lirakis harness will serve its wearer well for many years.

No matter which brand you own, the harness should be designed

A safety harness belongs in every sailor's kit, and a skipper should carry enough harnesses on board for every crew member. The Lirakis harness shown is of top quality. The knife and sheath and the ACR strobe light are valuable additions to the basic harness.

and worn so that, should you fall overboard, you will be towed with your head up and clear of the water. A harness that is too loose, or one that has its tether at your waist will tow you either head down or sideways—neither of which is desirable.

A six-foot tether will enable you to move around the boat attached to the jacklines and reach just about every point you need to. Yet there are times when you don't want a long tether, such as when you are working at the mast or outside the lifelines or pulpit. It is helpful, then, to have a second hook attached to the middle of the tether that can be used when a short length is all you need. This second hook will most often remain attached to the harness. When the full length is used, it is important to keep the middle hook free from snagging on deck gear.

The fully fitted safety harness should be snug but comfortable. If it is difficult to put on, uncomfortable to wear or a bother to use on deck, it won't be worn. Lastly, every crew member should have his own harness, which can be adjusted to fit and customized to suit each sailor's needs.

PROTECTION FROM THE WEATHER

Morale is a fundamental aspect of safety aboard a boat and nothing adversely affects a crew's morale as quickly and surely as being wet, cold, windblown and uncomfortable. When morale begins to fade, when the boat is no longer a happy ship, then mistakes will be made, judgment will err and small problems will gradually turn into large ones.

Just as important as morale is the threat to the crew from hypothermia. No matter where you sail, there will be times when the temperature and chill factor combine to lower your body temperature. Unless the crew is prepared to stay warm and dry, hypothermia can gradually immobilize them, again leading to errors in judgment and problems on board. If left to worsen, hypothermia can be fatal.

To protect yourself and your crew from the effects of weather and temperature, it is wise for each member of the crew to be fitted out

Use the layering method to stay warm and dry. The layer closest to the skin should be of a material such as polypropylene that wicks moisture away from the skin. Outer layers should block wind, rain and spray yet should also be of a breathable fabric, such as Gore-Tex.

with the appropriate clothing. How you prepare will depend on where you will be sailing, the types of winds you expect to meet, the night passages you will be making and the average temperature for the region.

Foul weather gear is the most essential item on the clothing list. There are a wide variety of suits available, yet the various styles are not designed to serve every purpose. Heavy insulated jackets and pants won't do in the tropics, and light tropical gear won't do you much good off the coast of British Columbia.

The advances in waterproofing technology over the past decade have been significant. Gore-Tex and similar breathable fabrics have changed the way we think of foul weather suits. It is now possible to own a suit that is virtually waterproof, yet will breathe enough to permit the evaporation of body moisture away from your body.

Whether you choose to go with the heaviest or the lightest gear, there are several aspects of foul weather gear design that set appropriate gear apart from the rest. A good suit should have welded or taped seams, an inner liner, pockets that remain dry, a collar to break the wind and a large, heavy nylon zipper. The better pants reach well above the waist, preferably to the armpits, and have suspenders, a large nylon-zipper fly, waterproof pockets and some reinforcing at the knees and on the seat.

Heavy suits, such as Mustang's Ocean Class one-piece suit, will not only keep you dry and warm, but have pockets for personal safety devices such as a small strobe, a miniature EPIRB and a whistle. Also, several of the suits in this category have enough flotation to qualify as life jackets, although they are not designed to keep the wearer's head propped above the water. In several of the suits, safety harnesses are sewn directly into the jacket.

In the medium range, the jacket and pants should be of moderate weight. The lining should be of light ventilated nylon. Pockets on the better models are waterproof and slit pockets are provided with warm polypropylene liners to keep your hands warm during cool night watches.

For sailing in the tropics, foul weather gear should be of light but waterproof material. Suits should be large enough to permit easy movement and the circulation of air around your body. In a tropical rain storm, moisture will build up inside the suit from perspiration almost as quickly as it does on the outside from precipitation. A suit made of a truly breathable fabric and one that has a well-ventilated inner shell will serve the wearer best.

If you will be sailing at night, it is important to have all suits fitted with strips of SOLAS-approved reflective panel. Top-of-the-line gear will come with the reflective patches sewn onto the shoulders, cuffs and hood. However, it is possible to add the strips and patches to your own suit. If a man is in the water, the patches will catch the light of a flashlight and greatly aid a search and rescue.

Keeping the crew in fit sailing trim involves more than just foul weather gear. What you wear under your suit will make the difference between being warm and really comfortable and being simply dry and cold. The best approach to undergarments has evolved in the mountaineering community. Companies such as Patagonia have developed new materials—synthetic fabrics that wick moisture away from the skin—and they have perfected the layering system.

In cold damp weather, two or three layers of warm, breathable undergarments beneath a foul weather suit will go a long way toward keeping you and your crew in a good frame of mind and safe from the ravages of hypothermia.

Beginning at the skin, a suit of light, synthetic long underwear will keep most of your body heat in while allowing body moisture to wick outwards. On top of the long underwear, a layer of heavier synthetic clothing—sweat shirt, sweat pants and so on—will trap the remainder of your body heat while absorbing the moisture that has wicked away from your body. Lastly, in truly severe weather, a top layer made from synthetic pile with an outer shell of Gore-Tex or another breathable fabric will serve to contain virtually all body heat.

The layering system works because it allows body moisture to flow away from your body while keeping body heat in. The layers should not fit tightly, for trapped air is a key ingredient in the system. Moreover, loose-fitting undergarments will permit greater mobility of your arms and legs and it is activity that generates the body heat that will keep you warm.

The last items that should be on the clothing list are hats and gloves. The old-fashioned wool watch cap still deserves a place of honor, for wool wicks away sweat while providing the warmth you want. If you intend to go completely high tech, hats knitted from synthetic fabrics will do the same job as wool.

Gloves are always a problem on a boat. Without them you will be able to handle lines and shackles, yet hands and fingers will gradually go numb. With them, your hands will stay warm, but your ability to work with sheets and shackles will be inhibited. In the last few years, polypropylene sailing gloves have come on the market that go a long way toward solving this dilemma. Light and warm, the gloves hug your fingers enough to permit some dexterity. More important, the new gloves dry quickly and provide a lot of warmth in little packages.

The well-dressed sailor is the sailor who is warm and dry, happy and active, no matter what the weather. If you plan to take your boat on longer passages or into areas where you can predict cold weather, then fitting out the crew in the right gear is as important as fitting out the boat.

SURVIVAL GEAR

Life jackets have long been required aboard all pleasure and commercial vessels. Yet life jackets are bulky, heavy and can get in a sailor's way as he is trying to handle a boat in rough conditions. For this reason, all too often sailors choose to leave their life jackets in the locker when conditions would dictate that they should be on a sailor's chest.

This is not a new problem. To seek a solution, the Mae West inflatable life jacket was developed. The first users were pilots flying over water who could not afford to have a full life jacket on them as they flew their planes, and couldn't afford not to be wearing a life jacket should the plane end up landing on the water.

The Mae West concept caught on in a big way in the 1980s when several new and unique life jackets and survival vests came onto the market. Possibly the most useful for sailors are the hybrid-type vests, which combine a safety harness with a tightly packed inflatable vest. Although somewhat bulky, the combination provides a

The new hybrid gear—combining a harness with an inflatable life vest—provides security without the bulk of a life jacket.

high degree of safety for any sailor working on a pitching foredeck. One such vest is manufactured by Mustang. It has an ORC-quality safety harness, with the addition of a sturdy crotch strap. The inflatable vest, worn around the neck like a horse collar, is quickly inflated by CO_2 cartridges and provides up to 35 pounds of flotation.

Several other similar vests are available on the market. Most can be manually inflated with tubes or rapidly inflated with CO_2, and some have automatic inflation systems. Inflatable vests will cost more than the combination of a harness and a life jacket. Yet the security they offer will make the cost seem nominal to those who want the latest in safety and survival gear. The main caveat when thinking about inflatable vests is the need to have the vests inspected from time to time and the need to maintain the CO_2 cartridges.

A simpler approach to the life jacket problem is the float coat. Although not approved as Type I or II devices, float coats combine the best of heavy foul weather gear with harnesses and flotation. A typical float coat will provide 16 to 25 pounds of flotation, depending on the size of the jacket. The flotation is built into the back and chest of the jacket, so the wearer will float faceup in the water. If you find yourself overboard without an injury, a float coat may be all you need to hang on until help arrives.

Better-quality float coats have harnesses built into them and are equipped with a crotch strap, reflective patches and pockets for a small strobe light, whistle and a miniature EPIRB. Perhaps the best thing about a float coat, emergencies aside, is the warmth and wind protection they provide. For those sailing in cold and rainy climates, a float coat can be considered standard sailing equipment.

The ultimate in safety apparel is the survival suit, which is carried by all commercial fishermen and mariners working in cold climates. A survival suit is a large, loose-fitting body glove that will keep a castaway sailor warm and afloat indefinitely, even in frigid waters. The suits come equipped with safety harnesses, inflatable life vests, reflective patches, a dye marker, strobe and a whistle. A personal EPIRB can be added for those going all out.

Survival suits pack up into bags that are the size of a small life raft. The sheer size of the suit makes them impractical for those sailing in smaller boats. However, if you have room aboard to store one suit for each of your crew and are seeking the ultimate in personal safety equipment, survival suits should be on your list. There are dozens of fishermen and commercial sailors who will tell you that this last line of defense is worth anything you have to pay for it.

THE SAILOR'S KIT

A crew—even if it is no more than a couple—is a team that goes out together to face, enjoy and prevail on the sea. As is the case with any team, there are certain essential pieces of equipment that each team member will need to do his or her best while on the water. You wouldn't send a baseball player out onto the field without his glove, hat, cleats and bat, and you shouldn't send your crew out sailing without their essential sailing kits.

In the previous pages we have covered safety equipment, clothing and survival gear in detail. What follows is a list of the items each member of the crew should own and carry aboard when heading out to sea.

- **Deck shoes.** At least one pair of deck shoes that provide sure footing and protection from toe stubs.
- **Foul weather gear.** A full suit suitable to the areas in which you will be sailing.
- **Safety harness.** A harness that fits comfortably and is strong enough and well enough made to keep the sailor on board.
- **Warm clothing.** Appropriate undergarments that will keep the crew warm, dry and mobile.
- **Rigging knife.** A pocket knife or holster knife that is sharp, easy to open and has a shackle key built into it.
- **Flash light.** A small, moisture-proof light, with spare batteries.
- **Hats.** A brimmed hat or visor to give protection from the sun and a watch cap to ward off the cold.
- **Motion sickness medicine.** Everyone gets seasick at some time or another and should be prepared if and when the time comes.
- **Sun block.** A supply of sun cream, zinc or other sun block to prevent burning from both the wind and the sun.

- **Sunglasses.** At least one pair of sunglasses that have polarized lenses and provide 100 percent protection from the sun's ultraviolet rays.
- **Gloves.** One pair of regular fingerless sailing gloves and one pair of warm, weatherproof sailing gloves.

EVERY SAILOR WILL have his own way of assembling the right items to go in his or her sailing kit. It is important that everyone on board know prior to setting sail that they are responsible for being well equipped, for keeping themselves warm, dry and in good sailing condition and, ultimately, for keeping themselves on the boat.

Chapter 6

SAFE BOAT HANDLING: SIX SITUATIONS

Docking and Mooring in Strong Winds
Sail Handling
Collision Courses
In Limited Visibility
Anchoring in Strong Winds
Running Aground

ONE OF THE delightful aspects of sailing is that it is a pastime that can engage a sailor for a lifetime. There are always new technologies, new gear and equipment to understand and new techniques to master. No matter how long you have spent at sea, there will always be fresh tricks an old dog can learn.

Boat handling is the practice of maneuvering and sailing a small or large sailboat in and around the confines of the coast. Often the situations that arise will be in tight quarters. There will be wind and currents to negotiate. There will be other boats and the crowd of commercial vessels that ply the waters between our great ports. And there will be the shore to sail close to, to anchor in its lee, to explore and ultimately to avoid bumping into.

As sailors gain skill and confidence, experience tends to teach many of the same lessons. While there are always new technologies and occasionally new techniques, the dictates of the sea and of the sailing environment remain the same.

Experienced sailors, particularly those who have undertaken long, shorthanded passages, share some basic approaches to efficient and safe boat handling:

Don't strain yourself or your gear.
Let the boat, the sails and the sea do the work.
Don't forget the obvious.

Safe sailing is about safe boat handling. There are a thousand distinct and different situations you can find yourself in as you explore the coastline and set off across open bodies of water for parts unknown. But the fundamentals of boat handling include safety aspects that can affect the well-being, morale and health of the crew. Here are six common situations that illustrate the thinking, planning and execution that make up sensible and safe boat handling.

DOCKING AND MOORING IN STRONG WINDS

Light and fluky winds are too often the nemesis of the coastal cruiser. But somehow inevitably, in our first situation, after a fluky morning and a fresh and rollicking afternoon, the wind really decides to pick up at just the moment you are trying to make your way into the dock or up to the mooring buoy.

The maneuvers close to shore or in other areas in which a sailor can get himself into trouble—a marina or anchorage—can be tricky. For sailors still new to the game, these maneuvers are often the most heart stopping of the day, precipitating the loudest shouts, the silliest mistakes and the most embarrassing moments. Without doubt, more unsafe incidents and boating accidents occur within a few hundred feet of the shore—or up against the shore—than anywhere else.

But there are simple tricks to making a success of the docking and mooring process that will enhance the safety of the crew and protect the boat from damage. The first is to remember to be alert to the obvious forces acting on you from the wind and the current.

The wind, if blowing hard, will usually be blowing from a constant direction. As you approach the dock or mooring, it can be your friend or your enemy. More often than not the choice is yours. You can choose to approach from the windward or the leeward side and you can use the force of the wind in the rigging to push you onto the dock or mooring, or into or out of a slip. You can't change the lay of the land, the angle of the dock or mooring you are approaching or

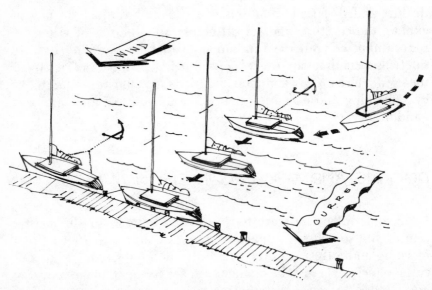

Docking downwind and down current: This is the least attractive way to come into a dock. If you must approach from this angle in bad weather, make certain you give yourself enough time and room to: (1) turn sideways to the wind and current and start to drift; (2) drop anchor; (3) drift slowly toward the dock, paying out anchor rode; (4) set the rode and stop the boat a boatwidth from the dock; and (5) set fenders and docking lines before permitting the boat to lie against the dock.

the direction of the wind. But you can change the way you and your boat approach under the circumstances.

Current, either the surface set of a strong breeze or the tug of a tidal or river current, will be a constant force against the keel of the boat. Like the wind, it will either be a help or a hindrance, depending on how you use its force.

So, study the obvious forces of wind and current before attempting to bring a boat alongside or up to a mooring. Once you have the two firmly in mind, then figure how they will affect the boat. A shallow, tall-rigged boat will bend to a breeze more than to a current. A heavy, deep, short-rigged boat will be gripped by a current and may not feel so sharply the force of the breeze. Know which situation belongs to you.

Once the basic lay of the land has been scoped out and the effects of wind and current are under control, it is time to lay a plan and rig docking lines and fenders, or mooring gear. Make sure the plan is communicated clearly to the crew, that everyone knows who is to handle which line, what they are supposed to do with them and the order in which all of the docking maneuvers will take place.

Remember that you do not want to put yourself and your crew in a situation in which brute strength on the end of a line or the mule power of winches is the only tactic. Don't strain your back or break your gear to get into a dock. Let the significant forces already acting on your boat do the work. The best onboard aid when docking, using the boat's force, is the spring line. If no other docking or mooring is rigged, a spring line, with judicious use, will bring you home. The next most important onboard item is patient planning.

There are three basic situations in which you will be maneuvering around a dock or mooring in a strong breeze and noticeable current. The wind and current will work you toward the dock, away from the dock or combine to neutralize each other. The maneuvers we will discuss are performed under power and at slow speed.

The Force Is With You

When approaching a dock or mooring on the windward and/or up-current side—the least-favored situation—ascertain where against the dock you want to position your boat. Once you have your bearings and a feel for the strength of the wind and current forcing you down on the dock, turn sideways to the wind and current and idle the engine. Slowly but surely you will drift down onto the dock, while you use the engine to move either forward or back to keep your chosen position in line.

The first line that should be made fast—or thrown to a helping hand—should be the spring line. If you want to move farther forward, instruct the line handler to tie off the spring line aft so you can slowly power ahead on it. If you want to position yourself astern, reverse the procedure.

When lying on the windward side of a dock in a strong breeze, laying out an anchor will help to hold you off the dock. Set the anchor so the scope will be at least five to one: five feet of line for every foot of depth. The anchor will be made fast either to an amidships cleat or to a simple bridle rigged from the bow and stern cleats.

If you have judged the point at which you should drop the amidships anchor and the point at which you should make your turn sideways to the wind and current with care, you will find yourself drifting gradually down onto the dock. As you draw near, begin to take a bite on the anchor rode to slow the boat down, make it fast and set it before you close to within a boat's width of the dock. As the anchor sets and the line stretches, you will find yourself lying very close to the pier, at which point the bow and stern lines and the spring lines can be made fast.

By proceeding slowly and deliberately, you have let the wind and the current do the heavy work, while you have done no more than handle lines, set an anchor and run the engine at slow revs.

Needless to say, in a strong breeze the windward side of a dock and the up-current side of a dock should be considered safe only in protected waters and only for a short time. In winds and waves that would cause the boat to bash dangerously against a pier, it is prudent to anchor off or find a leeward dock that will keep the boat and crew away from a possibly dangerous encounter.

The Force Is Against You

The safest situation in which to moor or dock a boat is against a dock or pier that provides a leeward side to the wind and a down-current side to the running current. But while lying to such a dock is the most comfortable and best for both crew and boat, making up to a leeward dock that has an offsetting current can be even trickier than falling down from the windward side, particularly in tight quarters.

The power of your engine and your ability to maneuver in tight quarters will affect your tactics during such an approach. If the way is clear and you can swing in a wide curve and approach the dock with enough forward momentum to bring the boat alongside where you want it, you will be able to make her secure quickly and surely. The trick is to tie off on an aft-running spring line first and then to continue to power ahead on it at low revs. The forward force of the boat combined with the aft tug of the spring line will force the boat toward the dock. Once close to the dock, the bow and stern lines can be applied and the boat secured. It is not uncommon in this situation to see an experienced skipper leave his engine in slow forward to keep the boat hard against her bumpers and the dock.

If you do not have room to maneuver, you will have to improvise. The easiest method is to run in on a long spring line. If you have no one to help on the dock, then run up to the dock bow first, drop off an agile crew—or more likely the only other person aboard—with the amidships spring line in hand. The spring should be made fast amidships and then played out from the dock as you back away and swing the stern into a position from which you can power ahead parallel to the dock.

Once you have powered aft into a position that is behind and just off the position you will fill on the dock, have the spring line made fast on the dock—well astern of the place you wish to occupy—and power forward at slow revs. The boat will move forward until it stretches the spring to its full extent; you hope you are now exactly parallel to and a couple of boat-widths off your spot. If not, adjust the spring line accordingly. From this position, continue to power ahead. The boat will ride against the spring and slowly slip sideways

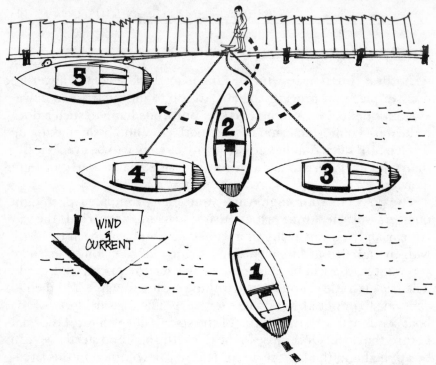

Approaching a dock upwind and up current, use the force of the engine and the leverage of a spring line to work your way up against the dock. (1) Approach the dock bow first and drop off a crew member with a spring line. (2) Back away to one side. (3) Steam forward past the docking spot, taking up strain on the spring line. (4) Continue to power ahead on the spring line, adjusting the rudder as necessary, so the boat eases sideways against the dock. (5) Continue to power ahead on the spring line while the rest of the docking lines are made fast.

toward the dock. You will have to play the rudder to keep the bow and stern even to the dock. Once up against the bumpers or the dock, you can arrange your bow and stern lines and set out breast lines to hold the boat close to the dock.

By using a simple plan and the force of the engine and the spring line, you can avoid backbreaking struggles hauling a boat against nature. With practice, you will gain confidence in the use of the spring line and in your ability to use it to muscle your boat into a tight mooring space.

The Force Is Against Itself

No doubt the easiest conditions in which to moor a boat are those in which the force of the wind against the rigging is nullified by the force of the current against the keel. Your boat will behave docilely and, even in unpleasant conditions, you should be able to make a standard docking maneuver without difficulty.

However, the real trick in such conditions is to read the current and the wind. When the two forces are running contrary to one another, the surface of the water will be roiled and difficult to read. How hard is the wind pushing? How swift is the current's set? It is important, even in this situation, to establish before closing in on the mooring just how both forces will affect your docking maneuvers. Don't forget that should another boat or a dockside building suddenly blanket the wind, the full force of the current might set you off in a direction other than the one you had planned.

Don't ignore the obvious around you: the strength of the current, the force of the wind, how these will play upon your boat, and how the factors around you will change those forces.

SAIL HANDLING

Whenever the wind begins to pipe up, whether on an afternoon day sailing or a longer passage, the crew's adrenaline begins to pump and the skipper finds himself at the juncture of a decision. Most often, as a gust of wind sends the rail under, everyone aboard will sense that the boat is overpowered and that it is time to reduce sail. As experienced sailors know, a boat that is overcanvased sails more slowly than one that has the right, reduced canvass aloft. Moreover, a boat that is overcanvased is more likely to suffer gear failure and crew injury than one that is being sailed to its optimum for the wind strength.

The old saw is to reef early and reef often. Following this simple rule will save wear and tear on your boat and gear, ease tension (and

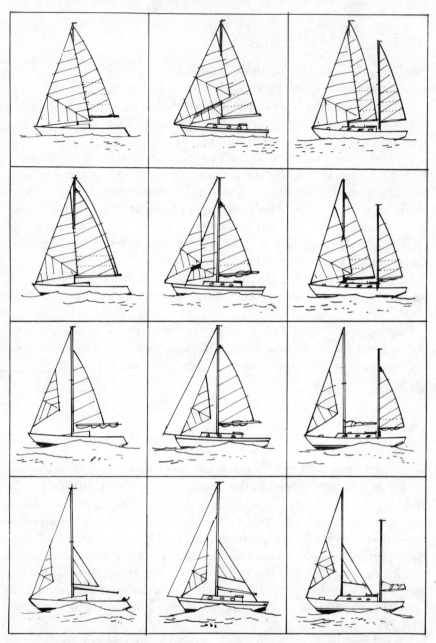

The standard reefing sequences for the three most popular sailing rigs.

thus heighten morale) among the crew, and ultimately put the boat and its crew in a safer position than if it carried too much sail too long.

When the wind is blowing hard, the pressure exerted on the sails and thus transferred to sheets, halyards and winches can be enormous, even in a small boat. It is important for the crew to know where all sheets are led and where the strains on lines and gear will be the greatest. Some skippers designate "red zones" around the deck where crew should not sit or stand because of the threat of a snapping sheet or a broken block. Even if no such red zones are officially designated on deck, every crew member should be aware of danger areas, particularly around genoa sheets, the main sheet and where spinnaker sheets pass through turning blocks. It may be obvious to avoid standing astraddle of a sheet under tension, but remembering and remarking on the obvious can avert a silly injury.

Changing Headsails and Reefing

On most masthead sloops, you will want to change down to a smaller headsail as the wind picks up and the boat becomes overpowered. With the new roller-reefing headsail systems, it is possible to roll in the sail. Normally the first reef will be approximately 30 percent of the sail area. The sail and roller system should be designed for reefing, with a foam luff pad that will keep the sail from bunching and a swivel on the system that will keep the head and tack of the sail even. As you roll in the sail, you will need to move the sheet lead car or block forward to keep foot and leach tension even. It is helpful to mark the foot of the sail at its reef points and mark the sail track at the corresponding position.

With roller-reefing headsails, it is possible to reduce sail area quickly and easily. However, the systems do require a crew member to leave the cockpit to move the sheet lead. Moreover, should the wind continue to rise, you will want to change down to a smaller jib or storm jib and doing so with a roller system can be extremely difficult. The large sail will have to be rolled all the way out and then lowered, without the restraining help of hanks on the headstay. In a strong breeze, controlling a big sail that is unattached can be difficult and possibly dangerous. Lastly, while the modern generation of roller-reefing systems has proved reliable, you may have no way to lower or roll up the sail should the device break down in difficult conditions.

Having considered the ease of handling and the possible problems, many sailors choose to use the roller systems and do so handily. Those who prefer to use the traditional headsail configuration may have fewer gear failures but will spend more time on the foredeck changing sails and will have to carry a wider compliment of headsails.

There are a few simple tricks that can save effort and time and increase safety when you are changing headsails. The first is to change down earlier rather than later. Avoid the strain of wrestling a big sail by lowering it before it becomes too big for one person to handle.

Always useful on the foredeck are sail ties with which to tie down a sail that has been lowered or has been prepared to go up. While under way, tie two sail ties to the stanchion bases on either side of the deck where they will be ready to make fast a sail.

Most modern cruising boats do not behave well under the main-

In a rising wind, head off and blanket the genoa behind the mainsail to simplify the headsail change. Once the new, smaller jib has been hanked on, raised and trimmed—all in the protection offered by the mainsail— you can head up again and continue on your way.

sail alone, so it is prudent to plan a sail change to reduce the amount of time you spend baldheaded or without a jib. Begin by hanking the new, smaller sail onto the headstay while the bigger sail is still flying. You may have to release the bottom piston hook to fit all the new hanks onto the headstay. The new sail should be tied along the windward side of the deck so it will be out of the way when the larger sail comes down.

If you are sailing upwind, you will find that the large headsail will be difficult to bring down as it flogs. It will tend to fly free of the foredeck and can easily fall overboard. To make the job easier, it is best to head off and blanket the sail behind the mainsail. With the mainsheet eased out and the jib sheet still somewhat tight, the big sail will luff easily and drop onto the deck as the halyard is released.

Once the sail is on deck, release the piston hooks from the forestay and then tie the sail down to the leeward deck with the sail ties already in place. Once the big sail is secure, remember to attach the tack shackle to the smaller sail, attach the jib sheets and move the sheet leads forward to the new position (which should be marked on the track); you are now ready to hoist away.

Be sure to clear the halyard from the forestay before you hoist the new sail. In rough conditions with the boat bobbing up and down, the halyard will whip back and forth aloft and can easily become tangled around a spreader or other protrusions up the mast. Also, make certain the halyard has not become wrapped around the forestay.

If your course is to windward, sheet in the jib before heading up to take advantage of the lee of the mainsail. Then, once the sail is trimmed more or less correctly, swing the bow back to windward and trim in the main.

While this procedure will lose you some ground to windward, the loss will be small compared to the benefits of working on a flat foredeck and having the jibs lowered and raised in the lee of the mainsail. Also, once you are back on course, more often than not the small sail will permit you to sail more efficiently into the wind and you will be able to make up lost ground quickly.

After reducing the size of the headsail, the next step, in a rising wind, is to reef the mainsail. If you have a Stoway mast or boom

(Stoway is the Hood Yacht Systems brand name, but there are other brands on the market) you will be able to ease off the main sheet slightly and then winch in your reef from the cockpit. On larger boats, the roller-reefing mainsail systems are a real boon to short-handed sailors and can save much stress and effort. Any owner of a larger sailboat should give careful consideration to such systems when rerigging a boat or installing a new spar. The slight loss in performance suffered by such a mainsail arrangement is more than compensated for by the ease and safety of using the rig.

Most sailors do not yet sail with a Stoway system and must use the slab or jiffy reefing system that is the standard on most boats. To use slab reefing safely and efficiently, it is vital that all reefing lines and reefing gear be in place and ready prior to setting out. Having to rig new reefing lines while under way is not only difficult, it can be dangerous.

To tame the main while tying in a reef, you may be able to simply release the sheet, let the main luff and quickly lower the sail to the reef points. It is helpful to mark the main halyard with indelible ink or a sewn seizing so you can cleat off the halyard after lowering the sail. Once the reefing cringle has been tacked down and the leech tightened, you can winch up the halyard again, and you're ready to get under way.

If conditions are particularly rough or if you have problems with the reefing system, the easiest approach is to heave-to and let the main out as far as needed. To heave-to, leave the small jib sheeted to leeward and simply tack. The jib will back and begin to force the bow away from the wind. Put the helm all the way down—tiller to windward or wheel to leeward—and the boat will virtually stop sailing and take up an easy position approximately 60 to 70 degrees off the wind.

Once the main has been reefed and you are ready to sail again, release the jib sheet, trim it to leeward and you are on your way.

When handling sails in rising weather, make sure the crew knows what needs to be done, how it will be done and where all gear and lines should be led. Don't try to force the sails or sheets and don't try to overpower the wind. It won't work. Use the sails and the natural lees they offer to make working on the foredeck or at the mast easier. By taking a little time, communicating clearly to the crew and

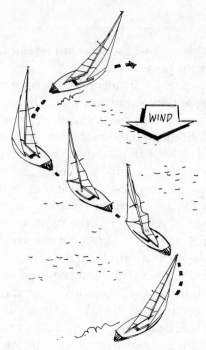

When reefing the main in rough conditions, you can slow the boat and ease its motion by heaving-to on a backed jib. Simply tack without releasing the jib sheet so the headsail fills aback. Lash the tiller to leeward (or wheel to windward). Let the mainsail out until it luffs and then reef it. Once the reef has been tied in, free the backed jib sheet, release the tiller and then trim the jib to leeward and continue on.

keeping the boat under control, you will find, even in a strong breeze, that sail handling can be accomplished without a lot of fuss and worry.

COLLISION COURSES

Most of us sail on weekends in harbors and bays that are becoming increasingly crowded. In the most popular sailing areas, it is not uncommon for several hundred sailboats to be out on a Saturday afternoon, all negotiating channels, trying to enter or leave marinas and mooring areas, and all sharing the same need to avoid bumping into each other.

Complicating this picture is the commercial traffic that will be heading to and from port, out fishing or transporting passengers. The commercial vessels will normally be operated by competent seamen. Yet, because they are making their livings on the water and are on the water every day, commercial seamen tend to put commerce ahead of politeness to the recreational sailor. Do not expect a fishing boat or ferry boat to get out of your way, and do not press your right of way against a ship. You might be able to win a court case should a ship run you down, but it will be a pointless victory.

It is important for all sailing in crowded waters to have a good working knowledge of the rules of the road, which we discussed in detail in Chapter 3. If there are novices aboard, spend a few minutes identifying the boats around you that have the right of way and those that do not. It can be fun on a crowded afternoon to place a wager or two on right-of-way situations to see if the skippers do the right thing or choose instead to make up new rules on the spot. Too often, rights of way are determined by bluster and ignorance rather than by following the established rules of the road.

For many sailors, sailing on a collision course with another vessel is the most stressful event of an afternoon on the water. Practice and experience will minimize the stress, but there still may be a few tense moments that hold the potential for an accident.

Determining that you are on a collision course is the first order of business. The standard test is to take a compass bearing on the other boat. This can be done with a handheld compass or a steering compass on the binnacle or in the cockpit. After taking the first bearing, wait a minute and take a second bearing. If the bearing remains the same, the courses of the two vessels will intersect. If the bearing changes forward on your boat, you will pass astern of the other boat; and if the bearing changes toward your stern, you will pass ahead of the other boat.

Another simple way to take a bearing is to line up two fixed points on your boat—a winch and a stanchion, for example—with the mast of the other boat. As long as you maintain your own course, the bearing from these two fixed points will give you the same information as the compass bearing.

Once you have established that you are on a collision course with another vessel, you will have to decide which vessel is the stand-on

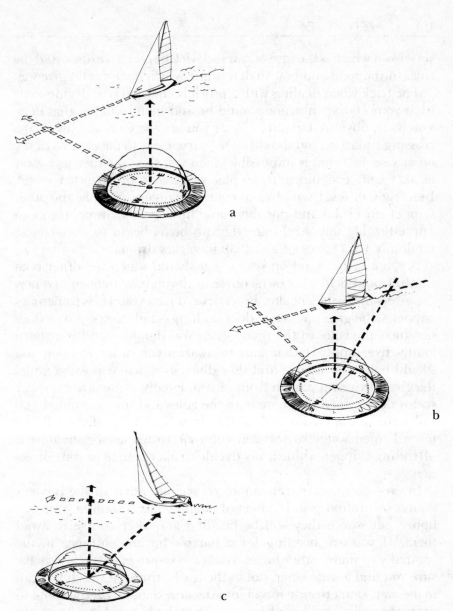

Collision Avoidance: Use a hand-bearing compass (a) or your main compass to take a bearing on the other boat. A few minutes later take a second
bearing. If the other boat is moving toward your bow (b), then it will pass
ahead of you. If the second bearing moves aft (c) then the other boat will
pass astern of you. If the bearing remains constant, you are on a collision
course and will have to react in accordance with the rules of the road.

vessel and which is the give-way vessel. In Chapter 3 we discussed the rules of the road and how to determine which boat should give way.

The trick when dealing with a possible collision is to decide early what your course of action should be and then to follow that decision in an obvious and sure way. If you are the give-way vessel in a crossing situation, you should alter course early to pass astern of the other vessel. If that is impossible, then you should either tack away or alter course significantly to pass well ahead of the other vessel. Indecision or less than obvious course changes can make the other skipper uncertain and possibly cause him to alter his course in an unpredictable way. And once the two boats begin to alter course randomly, the chance of a mishap increases dramatically.

If you are the stand-on vessel, you should watch the other boat carefully and hold your own course until you have determined how the give-way vessel will alter his course to pass you. If, as sometimes happens, the give-way vessel does nothing—fails to see you or does not know the rules of the road—then you should sound your horn loudly five times. If that fails to awaken the other skipper, you should hold your course and slow down as much as possible to let the give-way vessel pass in front of you. Finally, if the other skipper seems determined to ignore both the rules and your warnings, you will have to alter course significantly to avoid a collision. Do so toward open water so you can continue to maneuver should the offending skipper whimsically decide to alter course in your direction.

In crowded waters, remember to pay attention to the obvious goings on around you. If a fleet of racing boats is coming your way, figure out where they will be heading and alter course to avoid them. If you are heading for a narrow harbor entrance in the company of many other boats, assess the crowd early on and make sure you find a wide-open slot in the traffic through which you can maneuver. Don't decide to sail into the crowd and then round up to drop the sails. You'll confuse everyone. And, if fishing boats are working ahead on your desired course, remember that they may be hauling nets or pulling pots and will not be looking out for you. Give fishing boats a wide berth and, if possible, steer across their bows or well aft of their sterns to avoid tangling your keel in the nets.

If you know and follow the rules of the road, and if you operate your boat deliberately and surely, you will be able to avoid close encounters in crowded waters. But always remember to look out for the other guy. He just may be daydreaming.

IN LIMITED VISIBILITY

No matter where you sail, there will be times when you find yourself out on the water in limited visibility. You may run into a fog bank, you might be sailing on a particularly dark night, or you may encounter a torrential downpour. In each case, you will know the eerie sensation of losing your bearings as the landmarks and coastline vanish from view.

Becoming disoriented in poor visibility is a common malady that affects even experienced sailors. When the comfort of common reference points—whether a headland, buoys or the stars above—disappears from view and you are enclosed in a little world all your own, more often than not you will begin to mistrust both your navigation and your navigational equipment. It is easy to suddenly feel lost on the trackless sea.

The stress of such a situation can be more harmful to the crew than the hazards out there on the water. Disorientation can lead to confusion, poor judgment and silly decisions that can prove unsafe for both boat and crew.

When visibility closes down, remember that nothing around you has changed. The shoreline, rocks, buoys and other landmarks are still just where they were when you could see them. Moreover, if you had been trusting your compass to lead you to your destination when you could see ahead of you, it only makes sense to trust it when you can't see 10 feet. Too often, when the fog rolls in, the skipper or navigator will suddenly begin to doubt the compass and will conceive all manner of schemes to compensate for an imagined error. Doing so will only throw you into a navigational morass from which it can be difficult to extract yourself.

The importance of maintaining a regular and accurate dead-reckoning position becomes apparent when suddenly your visibility diminishes. If you haven't been keeping a DR log as you sail along on a fine afternoon, begin to do so as soon as you sense the weather closing in. Take bearings on familiar or known landmarks, take several depth readings to establish the bottom contour below you, and quickly plot the courses you will need to find your way into a safe harbor.

If you have electronic navigational aids on board, now is the time to establish how well they are working. If the loran, the depth sounder or the radar is giving reliable information while you can corroborate it visually, then, like the compass, the aids will continue to do so once you are blinded by the weather.

As you make these preparations, anticipate the traffic you might meet along the coast or in a harbor or bay. Larger harbors, used by commercial shipping, will have separation zones for in and out traffic. These will be noted on your charts. Make certain you will not be sailing smack in the middle of an opposing traffic lane. If you are sailing in a high-traffic area, tune in the VHF radio to Channel 16 and listen for "Securite" calls from other vessels. Also, switch over to Channel 13 from time to time to listen for radio traffic on the commercial operating frequency. Should you hear a vessel nearby, the thud of an engine or the whir of props, then use the radio to identify yourself, your position and your course. Such a call should follow the format: "Securite. Securite. Securite. This is the vessel *Nonesuch* [call sign] calling any vessel operating in the Mooki Channel. I am inbound, positioned at [give your latitude and longitude], sailing at six knots on a course of 255 degrees magnetic. Come back."

Along the coast in low visibility, the rules stipulate that you sound a horn every minute. It is just as important for you to listen carefully for other horns in your area. Should you find yourself on an apparent collision course with another vessel, it is prudent to slow down or stop to listen. It can be difficult to take a reliable bearing on a horn in fog or limited visibility. However, if you are stationary you will find that the other horn will begin to move to one side or the other. If it does not, and instead continues to come toward you, set a course to pass the unseen vessel port to port.

In such an encounter, remember that the other vessel will be steaming or sailing on a course between buoys or other landmarks. You may be able to estimate the vessel's course by comparing the bearings of his horn with known navigational marks in your area. Don't assume another vessel knows exactly where he is, but do figure that, like you, he is proceeding cautiously along a course that will maximize the safety of his boat and crew.

Sailing in poor visibility can be the bane of a coastal cruise. Yet, poor visibility can be handled and a cruise can continue, if you prepare for it in advance, keep your head and continue to trust the compass and other devices that have worked well while the sun was shining.

ANCHORING IN STRONG WINDS

Securing your boat at anchor when the wind is piping up can be a hair-raising experience. Even in relatively protected harbors, the surface of the water will be choppy, the boat will be bucking and veering in the wind, and communications between those in the cockpit and the person on the foredeck can be all but impossible. And it is often the case that anchoring is the last thing you do after a day of slogging through deteriorating conditions. You might be tempted to get the hook down, secure the boat and then hurry below.

Yet, if you pay careful attention to anything you do when faced with rising wind, you should give special care and concentration to laying out your ground tackle. Not only will you sleep better should the wind really howl in the night, you will also save yourself the confusion and possible danger of dragging.

When faced with a situation in which you have to anchor a boat in a high wind, you should first take careful note of the harbor and the surrounding shore. Take a good look at the chart to see where shoals lie and to figure where the current will be the strongest. When the wind is up, currents will tend to run faster, tides will tend to be higher and lower than normal, and the underwater hazards will present themselves at unexpected times.

In addition, take a careful look at the weather. Will the wind be swinging as the storm passes through and if so, which way will it swing? Will it increase during the night, or is the storm passing? Is

When anchoring in strong winds, choose your spot carefully, taking into consideration other boats, shoals, swinging room and possible danger to leeward should you drag.

rain in the forecast? And how long is the bad weather expected to last?

Survey the bottom to determine which anchors to use and how to deploy them. On the chart you will see indications of the bottom, whether it be mud, sand or rock. If you have the option, anchor in sand, which will give you the most reliable holding power and will accept the anchor without swallowing it the way mud does.

Select the spot to anchor by deciding where you will have the most protection from the wind from its present angle and from the likely angle should it shift. But pay attention to other factors as well. Don't anchor in a crowd. One of the boats to windward of you just might drag, fouling your anchors and damaging your boat. And make sure that downwind of your chosen spot there are no immediate hazards.

It will be tempting to drop all sail as soon as you enter protected waters and to maneuver under power alone. In tight quarters this will be the best solution, for you will be able to cut close circles if need be without having to manhandle the sheets. However, if you are anchoring in an open bay with enough room around you to make wide, slow turns, you may find that a reefed main or mizzen will act as a stabilizing force on the boat.

Before you begin your approach to the spot in which you will anchor, ready the anchor tackle. You should have two anchors ready if possible. If the bottom is muddy or sandy, you will want to use a lightweight or Danforth-type anchor and a plow. Both anchors should have lengths of chain and the chain should be attached to the nylon anchor rode with a swivel. If you have sufficient chain on board, use the chain with the plow and the nylon-chain combination with the lightweight anchor.

If you will be anchoring in rocky or grassy areas, you should have a fisherman-type anchor. The long, pointed fluke on this anchor will penetrate through grass into the sand below or hook securely in a crag in the rock. A fisherman anchor should be buoyed when anchoring in rock as it will have a tendency to lodge itself very securely.

In storm winds, or in the presence of a rising storm, you will want to set two anchors. The heaviest and most secure anchor should be set directly into the wind. This will insure that no matter which way the wind changes, either left or right, you will have your safest gear in front of you.

Once the first anchor has been set and a scope of at least five to one for chain and seven to one for nylon rode has been played out, take a look around you until you have your bearings. It will be vital, should you begin to drag, that you know exactly where you began. And while setting the second anchor, you will want to know fairly accurately where the first anchor is lying.

To set the second anchor, you have to have an idea of which way the wind is likely to swing. If the wind should move right, then the anchor wants to go to the right of the first anchor, and vice versa.

Power ahead with the helm hard over in the direction you wish to set the second anchor. If the main is still flying, sheet it in until it fills and you will quickly gather headway as you sail hard on the first rode. Continue pressing to windward until you have nearly reached the same relative distance upwind as the first anchor.

Set the second anchor at this point, and then fall back on the rode as freely as possible. It will be necessary to play out rode from the first anchor to make the set of the second anchor effective. Once you have set the second anchor, you will want to reset the first, which has been slightly worked on the bottom by the second maneuver. Drop off on the second rode and back down on the first until it is well set.

Finally, slack off on the two anchors until you are hanging be-

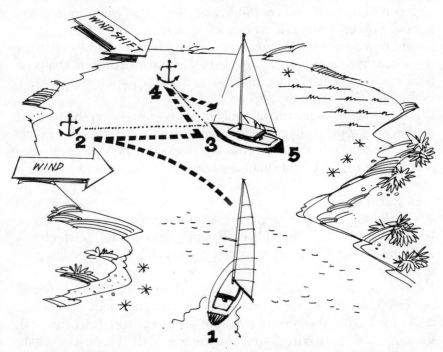

A second anchor should be set in the direction of the predicted or likely wind shift. (1) Choose your spot carefully, (2) set the first anchor, (3) then back down and prepare the second anchor, (4) steam forward to the spot where you will set the second anchor and (5) fall back onto both anchors and make the rodes secure.

tween them with a minimum of seven-to-one scope. In a breeze over 40 knots, you will find, no matter how protected the anchorage, that you will feel more comfortable with scope of 8 or 10 to 1.

Once you are settled down and have the sails furled and the boat tidied up, take magnetic bearings of your position. You will want to have two or three bearings on objects that will be illuminated at night, or at least on landmarks that are prominent enough to be seen even in darkness. Take your depth below your keel and figure the state of the tide or current; you may experience extreme lows and extreme highs and you will want to know where you stand.

Lastly, it is important to take precautions against the single most destructive force while at anchor in a high wind: chafe. Tape or tie chafing gear—elkhide, canvass, sailcloth, or even old blue jeans wrapped in duct tape—onto the nylon rode where the line passes through the bow chalk. Remember that the nylon will stretch a lot, so the chafing gear should cover the rode well inboard. The line may have to be taken up from time to time to keep the chafing gear at work.

On an all-chain rode, you will want to fix a nylon pennant and a chain hook. The hook, with a stout nylon line attached, should be hooked onto the chain, and then the chain should be let out until you have five or six feet of line running from the boat. The chain can now be made fast with a sag in it, and the nylon line can be made fast. The nylon will absorb the strain on the chain and will keep the boat from riding up on the anchor chain with a hard jolt. The nylon line attached to the hook should be fitted out with chafing gear exactly as was done for the nylon rode.

No one anchored in high winds sleeps well. But if you have equipped your boat with suitable anchors and rodes and have taken the trouble to set those anchors with care, you will rest a lot easier.

RUNNING AGROUND

Old salts who have spent time exploring the thin waters of the Bahamas, Chesapeake Bay or Cape Cod and The Islands will tell you that you haven't really cruised or experienced sailing if you

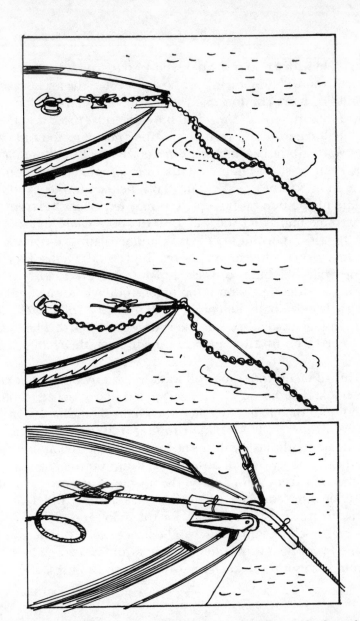

In strong winds, anchor rodes must be protected from chafe and from undue strains. On an all-chain rode, tie a length of nylon line into the last section of the rode to provide a shock absorber. A better solution is to use a chain hook attached to a length of nylon line. With a nylon rode, provide leather or plastic chafe gear to keep the fair lead or toe rail from sawing through the line.

don't run aground regularly. They are probably right, for if you are timid of the shore and afraid to nudge the bottom from time to time, then you will be hesitant to explore new bays or try a diversion up a narrow river.

To gain the confidence aboard your boat to go exploring in thin water, you will have to be confident of your ability to withstand a grounding and to get off again.

It is essential, however, before approaching a shallow harbor or bay to evaluate the danger involved should you go aground. Will you find yourself in breaking waves? Is the tide coming in or going out? If you get stuck, how long might you have to wait before the tide comes in again?

Once you have satisfied yourself that the way ahead is relatively safe and that running aground would not be a serious drawback, then go ahead and see what you can find in the alluring cove ahead.

As a general rule, the best time to approach a shallow entrance in which you might encounter the bottom is an hour or so before high tide. If you hit and then get stuck, you will have the last few inches of the flood and an hour or so to get yourself off again. Running aground on the wrong side of high tide can mean up to a 12-hour wait before the tide will float you off again.

The most useful piece of gear you will want to have on board during a grounding is an anchor that can be handled easily and has enough holding power and enough line to be used as a kedge. On larger boats, the main anchor and tackle may be too large and heavy for the purpose. Instead, a lighter lunch hook with sturdy but light tackle is the kedge of choice. An anchor that will either bury itself or hook a rocky bottom—such as a Bruce or a plow-type—may be the best all-around kedge to carry.

Grounding Under Sail

If you start to bump as you head into shallow water, immediately change directions toward deep water while striving to heel the boat to diminish its draft. If you were sailing into the wind, the best approach is to tack quickly. Leave the windward sheet attached and let it fill aback—on the backside—and keep the main trimmed in tightly. The bow will swing through the wind, you will heel sharply and, if luck and timing are with you, the keel will come free of the bottom. Once the tack has been completed, release the windward jib sheet and trim the headsail to leeward so you can sail off a bit to study the chart and the area around you more carefully.

If you are running and begin to bump, bring the boat hard on the wind as quickly as possible, either by heading up and trimming the sheets or by jibing and trimming. The choice will depend on the likelihood of deep water around you. If you have acted quickly and, again, have a bit of luck, you'll bump a few times and then be free.

If your quick reactions have not prevented the boat from becoming stuck on the bottom while under sail, don't panic. Remember that the boat's draft will decrease dramatically as she heels, so the first effort to get free should be to heel the boat as hard as possible and try to sail into deeper water. You can do this by overtrimming the sheets, hauling the traveler to windward and by moving the crew to the leeward side of the boat. Failing that, you will have to resort to more complex solutions.

The first option will be to turn on the engine and attempt to use its power to either forge ahead into deeper water or turn the bow toward the channel. But beware of overheating the engine. The saltwater intake will suck up the silt stirred up by the propeller, which can foul the engine's water pump. With the sails still flying, you will not be able to power backward toward the deep water behind you.

The second option, while under sail, is to use the kedge anchor. You should load the anchor and plenty of rode into the dinghy, leaving the end of the rode tied to the boat. Once you have rowed out into the deeper water, set the anchor. With the anchor rode led through a chalk at the bow and either to a windlass or aft to a cockpit winch, you can take up tension on the kedge. Now, trim the sails flat, move the crew to leeward and begin to take up on the kedge rode. The bow will slowly swing to deeper water and you can adjust the sails to heel the boat so you can winch her off. Once free, you can retrieve the anchor.

Running aground: When sailing up wind, as soon as you feel the keel nudging the bottom, tack and leave the jib sheeted to windward until you heel over, free the keel and are sailing in deep water again.

Grounding Under Power

More often than not, when you hit the bottom under power you will do so slowly, for normally you will be feeling your way into a tight cove or exploring outside the channel. Even so, you can get yourself really stuck at slow speeds. The first thing to do when trying to get yourself off a sandbank or rocky ledge under power is to pull in the dinghy painter. Nothing will complicate the already difficult situation more than wrapping the dinghy painter around the spinning prop.

Backing out into the deep water you know is behind you is the simplest and readiest approach. Put the engine in reverse and rev it. But again beware of sucking sand or silt into the raw water cooling system and don't push the engine over the red line. By moving the rudder back and forth quickly, you will be able to make the hull rock, which may just free the keel enough to let it slide backward.

If this approach doesn't do the job, you can set the kedge well behind you and run it either from the bow or the stern. With the combined power of the engine and the kedge, you can inch the boat off the sand.

As a last resort, or if you find yourself aground during a falling tide, you can greatly increase the heel of the boat by running the kedge well out into deep water and then hoisting the rode up the mast on a halyard. Attach a snatch block to the halyard and run the rode through it. Also, use a down haul of light line to retrieve the halyard should the rode have to be let go. Finally, before setting the kedge, attach an anchor buoy to it.

If you are stuck, set an anchor out in deep water rigged from the bow, then trim the sails in hard to induce heel, crank in on the anchor rode and slip off the mud.

If you are truly hard aground, you will have to heel the boat dramatically. Set a kedge anchor in deep water, run the rode through a snatch block that is hoisted up the mast and then crank down on the rode. The rode will crank the mast toward the kedge and will free the keel from the bottom. You will have to motor off if possible.

Once the kedge has been set, hoist the snatch block to the masthead, make the halyard fast and begin taking up on the anchor rode. If you do not have mast winches, use snatch blocks to lead the rode to a cockpit winch. You will be surprised at how quickly the boat will begin to heel over. With the engine in reverse (or forward, if deep water lies in that direction) apply revs and continue to take up on the rode. As she heels over, the keel will pull free of the bottom and you will begin to slide over the shallow spot that hung you up. Once free, you can retrieve the kedge and carry on.

Although running aground is a nuisance, it pays to make sure that everyone on board is familiar with the experience and knows how to get the boat off again. Unless the wind is high or there are immediate dangers to the boat and the crew, running aground is not a reason to radio the Coast Guard for assistance. You are on your own, and if you are prepared, calm and methodical, you will be able to get yourself sailing again in no time.

Chapter 7

MAN OVERBOARD

The Basics
The First 10 Seconds
The Quick-Stop Maneuver
The Jibe Maneuver
The Reaching Method
Using the Engine
Recovery Procedures
The Lifesling

No EVENT ON a boat, whether sailing in enclosed waters or in mid-ocean, is more traumatic and dangerous than losing a crew member overboard. The suddenness of a man-overboard emergency can freeze the brain and chill the heart. One moment you are sailing along, all is right with the world, all are happy and content on board. The next, calamity strikes. Adrenaline flows. Everyone on board struggles to a single purpose: Get that person back on the boat.

A great deal of the planning, preparation and practice that should be the prelude to safe sailing involves, first, keeping the crew on deck and, second, knowing how to react should a crew member

168

fall over the side. It is obvious that if you can keep the sailors on your boat safely aboard, you will never have to put into practice a man-overboard drill. Yet it is unfair to those who sail with you to assume that they will stay on board. If one does go over the side, all remaining crew must know how to react, must be well versed in the man-overboard drill and must know where all man-overboard equipment is stored and how to use it. The key to recovering a man in the water is practice. The best equipment and a theoretical plan will not be of much help if no one knows how to employ them quickly and decisively.

THE BASICS

There are some very basic axioms designed to keep sailors on board that should be often repeated and thought about by all who sail on open water. A responsible skipper will not assume that his crew has thought these items through, nor will he assume that saying them once will suffice.

Men never urinate over the side at night or in bad conditions. It is a fact that most sailors pulled from the sea after lengthy and expensive search and rescue missions—missions in which Coast Guardsmen and other sailors have risked their lives—are found with their flies open.

Don't take stupid chances. There is little place aboard a sailing boat for machismo. Don't think that heroics in the rigging or daredevil tricks outside the lifelines or over the side of the boat are a matter of course on a boat. They're not. It is almost always possible to retrim the sails or alter the boat's course to a more favorable heading before attempting a risky job on deck. If you have to go to the end of the boom, up the mast, or out to the end of the spinnaker pole, do so with planning, caution and the backup of everyone in the crew. And always protect yourself with a harness or a safety line.

Don't hurry. There is seldom a good reason to run anywhere on a sailing boat. There are even fewer reasons to act in a mad hurry. If you and your crew are sailing under control and know how to control the boat even when an apparent crisis arises, you will be able to react calmly and surely. Don't hurry. Think first and then act prudently.

Stow lines and gear safely. Nothing is more dangerous in poor conditions or at night than sailing on a boat that is cluttered with loose gear, badly organized and littered with tangles of uncoiled lines. On such a boat, every step can lead to a trip that could send you overboard. All gear on the foredeck and cabin top should be securely tied down and positioned out of the way of working crew. All lines, either halyards at the mast or sheets in the cockpit, should be coiled and secured out of the way of moving feet. Spinnaker poles, life rafts and dinghies carried on deck all must be securely tied down to the deck and must be arranged so they are out of the way of the working crew.

Don't procrastinate. In deteriorating weather, it is natural to assume things will get better and to wait to reef or to tend deck chaos until things get better. In fact, when the weather begins to deteriorate, things always get worse before they get better. When you first think it is time to reef, when you first realize deck gear is getting loose, and when you first get an inkling that a dangerous situation might lie ahead, then it is time to act. To wait is to invite a situation in which you are working on deck in bad conditions—the most likely time for a man to go over the side. To act quickly and early is to anticipate a worsening situation and to forestall it.

Wear your harness. It is common on boats sailing with children for the small people to be required to wear their harnesses whenever out of the cockpit. This rule should apply to all crew members as soon as the wind picks up, as soon as darkness falls and as soon as the crew begins to make noises about reefing. A harness is not a symbol of weakness. A harness is a badge worn by those who know the difference between a small hassle (the harness) and a big one (the sight of the transom sailing away).

THE FIRST 10 SECONDS

A boat traveling at six knots is moving through the water at approximately 10 feet per second. In the time that it takes you to read this paragraph, a person who fell over at the first word will be at least 50 feet behind you. If you stop to think about it, he will be 100 feet behind you. And if you don't know what to do next, if you freeze, he will be 200 feet behind you.

What you do in the first 10 seconds of a man-overboard situation will determine the outcome of the emergency.

At the instant you know a person is over the side the first thing you must do is shout—very loud and clear—"Man overboard." Have no doubt that this will get the rest of the crew's immediate attention. But don't be bashful. Shout it three times.

The instant you begin to shout, also begin to count in seconds. You may need to know later just how far you sailed from the point the person went into the water.

Immediately, as you are sounding the alarm, throw a flotation cushion to the person in the water. Don't panic. Throw it as accurately as possible. You will probably have aboard a man-overboard pole attached to a horseshoe buoy. Although you may be tempted to release the pole at this point, remember that it will take you up to 30 seconds to get the whole rig deployed, by which time you will be 300 feet from the person in the water—where the pole and horseshoe will do him little good. Instead, keep the pole aboard and plan to use it in the pickup maneuver if necessary.

If there are other people on deck, assign a spotter. The spotter should take up the count and should be the person who knows what course you were sailing at the moment the crew member went over the side. He should point directly at the person in the water and never take his or her eyes or pointing arm off the person.

The first 10 seconds are racing by. It is time to make the pickup maneuver that will get the man in the water back again as quickly as possible.

THE QUICK-STOP MANEUVER

A lot of thought and study has gone into the problem of the best way to recover a man in the water from the deck of a sailboat. A combined effort by the United States Yacht Racing Union Safety at Sea Committee, the U.S. Naval Academy Sailing Squadron, the Cruis-

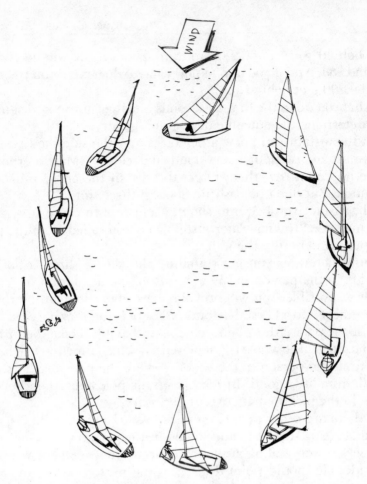

The Quick-Stop Maneuver: As soon as you shout "Man overboard" and throw a life cushion to the person in the water, initiate the Quick-Stop Maneuver. It is designed to keep the victim in sight and the boat always under control.

ing Club of America Technical Committee and the Sailing Foundation of Seattle has generated what is known as the "Quick-Stop" method.

The basis of the Quick-Stop recovery method is to stop the boat as quickly as possible. The shorter the distance between the man in the water and the boat, the better the chances for a swift and safe recovery. In fact, there is a strong correlation between losing sight of a victim and the fatality of that victim. The Quick-Stop method keeps the victim in sight at all times.

1. Once you have shouted "Man overboard" and thrown a cushion to the person in the water, immediately head the boat into the wind, no matter what angle of sail you were on. Bring the bow through the wind and let the headsails back, even a spinnaker.

    Studies determined that taking the time to deploy the man-overboard pole would delay the Quick-Stop. It is therefore recommended that the pole and horseshoe bouy be reserved for deployment should the first pass at recovering the person in the water prove unsuccessful.

2. Once you have tacked, continue to head away from the wind until the wind is aft of the beam. Hold the beam reach for two or three boat lengths and then begin to head directly downwind.

3. Drop the headsail once you are headed downwind.

4. Under mainsail alone, sail downwind until the person in the water is aft of the beam. Then jibe and slowly head up toward your target.

5. It is best to approach the person from the leeward side at an angle of 45 to 60 degrees off the wind. Your intent is to stop the boat a short distance to leeward of the person and make contact with a heaving line. If you stop to windward of the person, you run the risk of running over him as you make leeway.

6. Once contact is made, you should begin the process of bringing the person on board.

The Quick-Stop method has proved itself in numerous tests and trials. One of its main advantages is that it can be undertaken by one person at the helm without the need of other crew. Additionally, the method will bring you back to your overboard crew faster and in better control than other methods, while permitting you to keep the victim in sight at all times.

THE JIBE MANEUVER

Similar to the Quick-Stop method, the more traditional method of picking up a person in the water involves making a quick circle and returning to the person from the leeward side. The only difference lies in the first maneuver. Instead of immediately heading into the wind to stop the boat, you immediately head off away from the wind, jibe the mainsail and head right up into the wind again. As you are coasting to windward, drop the jib.

If performed smoothly, and if the spotter is calling the position of the person in the water, it is likely that the boat will come to a stop just to leeward of the person in the water.

It is important to keep the boat under control and to cut a circle through the jibe that will bring you to a stop before overrunning the victim. Once the boat has come to a stop, make contact with the victim with a heaving line and begin the recovery process.

The main drawbacks to the jibing method—and the reasons the Quick-Stop was developed to replace it—are that jibing is a more difficult maneuver to control; it drives the boat away from the victim and forces it to accelerate; it can do serious damage to the rig (including dismasting the boat); and it can create a serious threat to crew members on deck.

The jibing method should not be considered the recovery method of choice. However, if you sail a vessel that cannot tack efficiently in strong or very light breezes, or if you are sailing without a headsail and thus will have difficulty tacking, you may opt for the jibing method.

Sailors who have been on the water for years and who learned the jibing method as children or in sailing school should consider it one more tool in the bag of possible methods to recover a victim in the water. But every sailor should take the time to learn the Quick-Stop maneuver. It is better in every way than other recovery methods, no matter how venerable those methods might be.

THE REACHING METHOD

The reaching method of recovering a person in the water is the least efficient, least effective and least desirable way to maneuver a boat in a man-overboard emergency. Although it is still taught by reputable sailing schools and still has credibility as a traditional tactic, the reaching method should be considered the worst of the three options. We discuss it here only because it is still taught widely and because there are some built-in dangers that should be pointed out.

The intent of the reaching method is to keep the boat in the same position relative to the victim while controlling sails and handling the boat.

1. As soon as you hear "Man overboard," toss the flotation cushion and then turn the boat directly onto a beam reach and mark your new compass heading. It is essential for the helmsman or the spotter to begin counting seconds immediately.
2. Drop the headsails and secure them on deck.
3. Once the boat is under control, tack the boat and sail on the reciprocal heading. Note the seconds counted on the first leg and sail until you have covered the same ground on the way back. Take careful note of your speed and sail the same distance, not simply the same number of seconds.
4. At the mark point at the end of the second reach, stop the boat and make contact with the victim with a heaving line. Now you can begin the recovery process.

The problems involved in the reaching method involve the vagaries of timing, speed, leeway and the drift of the person in the water. It is essential to have a spotter who will keep his eyes on the victim at all times. Also, it is extremely important that the helmsman or navigator calculate time and distance as accurately as possible.

Performing the reaching maneuver under any duress, such as the panic a crew would be enduring when one member has fallen overboard, is very difficult. The maneuver requires a cool head, an ability to perform calculations and very careful boat handling. None of these things is likely to be possible in an emergency. The method also requires at least four able crew, all of whom are performing at their peaks. Very few cruising boats ever sail with such a complement.

USING THE ENGINE

Turning on the engine may be a useful aid as you maneuver back to the victim in the water. However, there are several risks involved that need to be considered before you set the propeller in motion beneath the hull.

In a moment of emergency, it is common to overlook lines and sheets hanging over the side. Yet should you inadvertently tangle a sheet around the propeller, you can complicate an already difficult situation. First, a tangled prop will render the engine useless should you need it later in the rescue. Second, as the prop winds the line tightly around the shaft, it is possible to spring the stuffing box and open a serious leak into the boat. And, lastly, when you are maneuvering the boat close to the victim in the water, a spinning prop is a real hazard that can do serious injury to the already traumatized crew member.

While the engine may prove extremely useful, particularly if you need to gain ground quickly to windward, it should be handled with care and a cool head. If it is not, further disasters could await you.

RECOVERY PROCEDURES

Once you have completed your recovery maneuver, a Quick-Stop, a jibe or a reach, you must make initial contact with the person in the water. ORC recommendations stipulate that a heaving line be handy in the cockpit. Several lines are commercially available that will do this job satisfactorily. It is vital, at this juncture, that the boat be under control and that the heaving line be thrown accurately.

In a strong breeze it will be difficult to throw the heaving line into the wind. If the engine is running, make certain that the line does not get tangled in the propeller.

If contact is made with the victim on the first throw, the crew should haul the person in the water to the boat. On smaller boats, you will be able to hoist the victim into the cockpit or he will be able to pull himself on board. However, on larger boats with high topsides you will need to use another method.

If the sea is calm, you may be able to attach the swimming ladder to the side of the boat and help the victim climb aboard by himself. But in rough weather a ladder can be difficult to attach and will be difficult to climb.

If the person in the water is injured or the topsides are too high for you to haul the person onto the boat manually, you will need to fashion a sling that can be fitted around the victim's chest and attached to a halyard. A docking line or jib sheet can be quickly knotted with a large bowline at one end, which is then slipped around the victim. A second bowline should be tied into the line and then the main halyard attached. With the aid of the halyard winch, you can hoist the victim on board.

Although such a recovery method may seem simple on paper, it is fraught with dangers for the person in the water and is more than likely to fail on the first or second attempts. Aware of this problem, the organizations that developed the Quick-Stop method also developed a simple, standardized method for getting the man overboard attached to the boat and then back on deck quickly and safely.

THE LIFESLING

In an effort to simplify picking up a person in the water, the organizations that developed the Quick-Stop method sought a way to make the pick-up maneuver a standard extension of the stopping maneuver. Realizing that relying on a heaving line to make contact with the victim was chancy and that fashioning a sling could waste precious moments, the group developed one piece of gear that could accomplish both tasks.

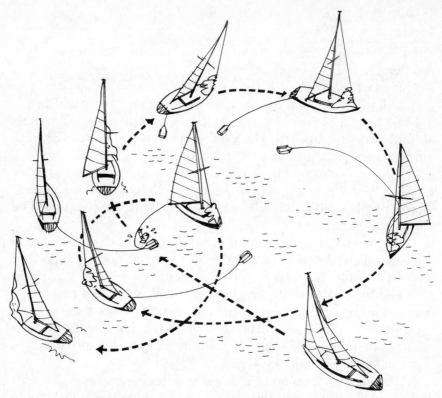

When using the Lifesling to pick up a victim in the water, first perform the Quick-Stop Maneuver. When you are approaching the victim, stream the Lifesling out behind the boat and then circle the victim closely so he can grab the sling. Once you have the victim attached to the boat with the sling, drop the sail and stop the boat.

The Lifesling, which is the brand name for what generically is known as the Seattle Sling—it was developed by the Sailing Foundation of Seattle—combines a long line with a buoyant horseshoe-type collar that doubles as a hoisting sling. When not in use, the Lifesling is stowed in a neat package fixed to the stern pulpit, where it can be deployed quickly by the helmsman. To use the Lifesling:

1. Complete the Quick-Stop maneuver as described above. As you approach the person in the water at an angle of 45 to 60 degrees from the wind, drop the Lifesling into the water and let it trail behind.

2. Sail to leeward of the victim, passing about a boat length away. Once the victim is astern of the boat make a wide turn into the wind, tack and immediately head off again to complete a circle around the victim.

3. The victim should grab the Lifesling line as it passes and hang on while the boat completes its circle.

4. The boat should be stopped head to wind, and the mainsail dropped.

5. With the victim attached to the boat via the Lifesling, haul him in and pull him aboard as quickly as possible. If the topsides are not too high and the victim is not seriously injured, you will most likely be able to manhandle him into the cockpit.

6. In a situation in which you are not able to lift a person onto the boat, you may have to use a block and tackle to hoist him

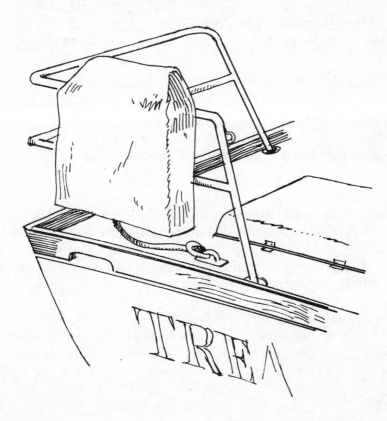

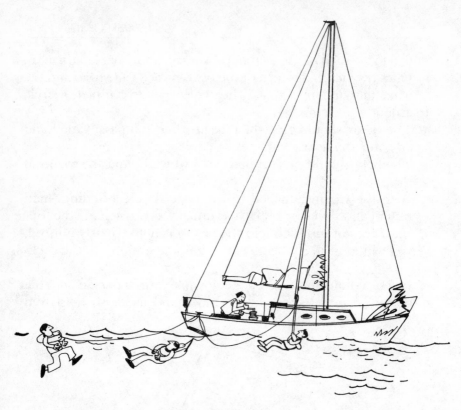

The Lifesling is designed to be worn under the victim's arms and around his chest. The sling has D-rings attached to the floating collar. To retrieve a heavy person, attach a halyard or a block and tackle to the D-rings and hoist the person aboard with a mast or cockpit winch.

aboard. Attach the block and tackle—one is available with the Lifesling—to the main halyard. Hoist the halyard about ten feet off the deck and then attach the tackle to the Lifesling. Using the block and tackle and winch power, you can then hoist the victim onto the boat.

A man-overboard emergency may be the most serious crisis you ever have to face while sailing. To be ready if and when the time comes, it is important that you prepare your boat with the appropriate equipment, that you plan the maneuvers you will use and the rescue techniques you have prepared for with the crew and, lastly, that you practice the man-overboard drill until all on board know exactly what to do.

Your life or the life of a family member or friend could one day depend upon your ability to act surely and efficiently in a moment of crisis.

Chapter 8

HEAVY WEATHER SAILING

THERE IS A certain pleasure seasoned sailors find in remembering and recalling for their friends their experiences of heavy weather at sea. For the most part, experienced sailors will not brag about weathering a gale. They will not hold forth, while leaning on a safe mantelpiece before a homely fire, and instruct the unknowing and unwary. But among like-minded people, among those who have been out there when the wind blows the waves white and black, when the roar of the wind is a freight train in the ears, among those who know, there is a sense of kinship. And kinship engenders stories. Some true. Some exaggerated. Some apocryphal.

The sharing of experiences is the desire to compare and the

desire to say, Yes, I've been there and it is more amazing than anything else.

Very little on land bears comparison to a gale at sea. If you have ever been caught close to a raging forest fire, you will understand the ferocity of a gale at sea. If you have ever been trapped on a mountain side by a sudden blizzard of snow, you will understand just how small you can feel. A gale at sea shows the force of nature, stripped naked of all its civilized apparel.

To weather a gale is no small feat. Yet every sailor who sets out to sail far along a coast or to cross a wide patch of open water will eventually meet high winds and heavy weather. Such conditions are not the reason for going to sea. They are the risk. And in that risk lies some of the simple challenge of going sailing and the fundamental appeal of facing the sea, one-on-one, in a sturdy craft and

Roger Swanson's *Cloud Nine* blasts down a North Atlantic roller during a transatlantic passage, sailing under control with only a small headsail sat.

with an able crew. In bad weather, you hold your fate in your own hands. The vast majority of the time you will be successful and the success is yours alone. Should you fail, you have the satisfaction of knowing no one else is to blame.

Sailing safely depends upon the self-reliance of the owner, the skipper, the person in charge. At no time on the water does that simple premise demand more than when the wind pipes over 40 knots and the sea begins to break in black-and-white streaks of foam.

A HEAVY WEATHER ATTITUDE

When the weather report or the change in the sky alerts you to an impending patch of bad weather, it is important to begin your preparations. How the crew anticipates the high winds and possibly high seas ahead, how they keep their composure and react quickly to changing situations will be a determining factor in how you and your boat weather the storm.

The skipper's attitude and the attitude of the crew will make the difference between a well-run, safe ship and a poorly run, unsafe one.

The first order of business is to allocate clearly the specific areas of the boat for which each member of the crew will be responsible. If there are only a few on board—even just a couple—the various duties required before sailing into heavy weather should be divided among the crew and a schedule established.

The skipper will be responsible for the overall performance of the crew and will, more than likely, also have to take on several areas of preparation, depending on his experience and skills.

Once the duty roster has been established and a schedule set for completing prestorm preparations, it is wise for the skipper and/or the navigator to show everyone on board where the boat is on the chart, where the storm center or front is likely to pass and what the various course options will most likely be before, during and after the storm. If the crew is well informed and capable of carrying on should the navigator become disabled by seasickness or injury, they will be happier, more confident and better prepared to do their parts in running a tight ship.

The greatest danger during periods of high winds comes not from the forces of the sea and the wind alone, but from the gradual deterioration of the condition and morale of the crew. Should gear begin to break, should several vital members of the crew take to their bunks with sickness, should those in charge of the galley fail to provide nourishment, then exhaustion can overtake those still sailing. Poor decisions can be made. Reactions to changing wave and wind patterns can be slow and erratic. And, finally, a sense of despondency can overtake the boat. In such a state, the crew is no longer acting as the master of the situation but the victims.

It is important for the skipper to anticipate who will be strong, who will most likely become sick and who is prone to panic. By addressing these potential problem areas early in the preparations prior to a storm, you can go a long way to heading off a dangerous situation. No skipper can afford to be left alone on deck while a frightened and seasick crew hides below.

There may be no better way to help those who could be liabilities during poor weather than to involve them actively in the preparations early. Delegate authority and allow each crew member to remain active, busy and committed. Engender a sense of confidence by listening to each person and by explaining instructions calmly and clearly. The safety of the ship and the crew belongs solely to the skipper. But if he carries all the weight of that responsibility on his shoulders alone, he will tire and possibly break, while the crew frets and hides below.

A heavy weather attitude is one that is full of confidence in the boat, respectful of the forces of nature to be confronted and calmly decisive when the going gets tough.

PREPARING THE BOAT AND CREW

Setting up the duty roster in the hours before the onset of bad weather—assuming you have the luxury of time—should be done with attention to the strains that will be put on the boat, the gear that could fail, the safety of the crew on deck and below and finally the crew's general well-being. Split the responsibilities into the following categories:

- Standing and running rigging
- Deck stowage, jacklines, weather cloths and cockpit
- Engineering: engine and systems, plumbing and batteries
- Navigation and communications
- Food and crew well-being

On most boats, the preparations listed above will fall to two or possibly three people. Time will dictate just how comprehensive the prestorm preparations can be, but no matter how short the time—unless you are surprised by a sudden line squall—you should be able to run through the boat's systems rapidly and get both the boat and yourselves ready to withstand the deteriorating weather ahead.

Standing and Running Rigging

Start with the standing rigging and check all stays, turnbuckles, and swagings for cracks or other damage. Look for exposed cotter pins or other sharp objects and tape them over with self-amalgamating tape. If the forestay has too much play, tighten the backstay slightly to take up the slack; this will have the additional benefit of flattening the set of the mainsail. If you have running backstays, set them up.

The running rigging should be checked for wear and tear. Look for chafe in the main and jib sheets and replace them or swap them end-for-end if necessary. Inspect the mainsail for wear or small tears. If time allows, you may be able to affect small sail repairs—with sail tape or sailcloth and contact cement—which will keep the main from ripping in a high wind. Stow unused sails below and prepare the storm jib and storm trisail for use.

Deck Stowage

Any gear that is stowed on deck that can be moved below, should be. A life raft and dinghy will have to remain on deck and the lashings should be checked and doubled if necessary. Anchors stowed on deck or in bow rollers should be securely tied down.

If the jacklines on deck and in the cockpit are not already rigged, set them up and test them. Make sure a life-harness hook can slide unencumbered from bow to stern.

In the cockpit, stow below any nonessential gear, such as a cockpit table or cooler. Tie sail stops on either side of the cockpit as handholds for the crew. Set up the weather cloths around the cockpit to protect the helmsman and crew from the wind and spray. Make certain the winch handles are in place and that a spare handle is readily available below.

Engineering

Check over the entire engine installation and the systems related to it. Top up the oil and coolant and check for any leaks in the cooling and exhaust plumbing.

Charge the batteries to capacity and make sure the batteries are well secured. Double the lashings if you are in doubt.

Check all pumps to make sure they are in working condition. The bilge pumps should have strainers in the bilge. These should be inspected and cleaned. Inspect the bilge to make sure there is no debris that could block a bilge pump. Lastly, pump the bilges dry.

Inspect all the boat's sea cocks to make sure they are in working condition and that the wood emergency plugs are handy should a sea cock fail. If the plumbing attached to the sea cocks has not been attached with double hose clamps, now is the time to add the second clamp.

Take a look at the steering system and check the cables for tightness. The wire leads from the wheel should be running smoothly through the turning blocks. Make sure the sheaves are in good condition, that the bulldog clamps on the cables are secure and that the whole assembly has been adequately greased. Inspect the quadrant for possible cracks. Finally, check the rudder post through-hull to ensure that there are no cracks in the hull and no water weeping in around the post.

Navigation and Communications

As soon as possible, get the best fix on your position as possible and then double check it. Any electronic aids—such as RDF, loran or radar—should be switched on, checked and any problems noted.

Set up a procedure to log entries every hour, making certain anyone making an entry lists course, speed, wind strength, sea state, barometer reading and temperature. The navigator should update the DR position on the chart at least once every watch, if not hourly.

Establish which radio frequencies will give you the best weather information for your area and post both the frequencies and the times of broadcasts next to the radio receiver. Also, check the time signal (WWV or WWVH) and note any errors in the on-board navigational clock.

If ship traffic is in the area, contact them on Channel 16 and alert them to your position, your course and your speed. You may also wish to set up a radio schedule with either a shore station within broadcast distance or a ship or other vessel in the area.

Food and Crew Well-Being

At the first indication of bad weather, everyone on board who is prone to seasickness should take their medicine of choice. The boat should be stocked with several different types of antiseasickness medication, but it is important that each crew member know what works best for him and carries that as part of his sailing kit.

Hot food should be prepared before it becomes difficult or impossible to work in the galley. Thermoses filled with soup, cocoa, stew and coffee will remain hot for up to 12 hours and will provide a tired and cold crew with the pick-me-up they need after a turn on watch.

It is helpful to have sandwiches premade and stored in a convenient locker for ready access. If things get too rough even to drink soup, a peanut butter sandwich will give the sailors the lift they need. Other snack food should be made ready for those on watch. Candy bars will provide energy and granola bars will help to fill an empty stomach. For those suffering from seasickness, have dry crackers, such as Saltines, at hand. A bottle of fresh water should be handy to help stave off dehydration.

Once food has been prepared, the person in charge of the galley should make sure that all lockers in the galley and saloon are secure and their contents stowed to prevent damage. Any objects that could become dangerous projectiles—the lids of the ice box, floor-boards, the batteries, the galley stove and so forth—should be either stowed away securely or fixed in place with barrel bolts, positive latches or even duct tape.

The crew should each have an assigned berth and should have their lee cloths tied in place. It is common on modern boats to find only one or two berths that can be considered "sea berths," so you may find yourself sharing your berth with the other watch. It is critical when sharing berths that each member of the crew do his utmost to keep the berth dry, neat and warm. Nothing is worse than coming off a cold night watch only to find your sleeping bag soaked, your gear scattered and the cabin in disarray.

The crew member in charge of the galley should be the enforcer of cabin neatness, particularly in bad weather. Any mess that occurs—spilled food, cooking oil, engine oil—should be cleaned up immediately to prevent others from slipping. Clothing should be stowed in lockers and never left lying about the cabin. When coming below in wet foul weather gear, remove the gear at the bottom of the companionway ladder or in the head to prevent the cabin from getting damp. Don't come below dripping and stand around in the saloon, dripping on cushions and the floor. Keeping the cabin dry and warm will do much for crew morale. A damp cabin soon becomes very uncomfortable.

Once you have completed preparing the boat and crew for heavy weather, you will have had a good look at all of your vital gear, stowed the boat tightly, battened down on deck and anticipated what could go wrong. Not only will such preparations secure the boat for bad weather, the process will give the crew the confidence and the sense of teamwork they will need to get through bad weather without a mishap.

STORM SAILS

As the wind pipes up and you and the crew feel the boat being overpowered, you will have to begin to shorten sails. In Chapter 6 we discussed the basics of reefing and some techniques to make the job

If you will be sailing in areas frequented by gales, storm sails are a must. Be certain you know how to rig and set your storm sails before you find you need them.

easier and safer. But when the wind really begins to howl, when it holds steady at 30 knots or more and gusts above that, the time has come to shorten down to storm canvass.

Most coastal sailing boats will not be equipped with dedicated storm sails—the spitfire jib and storm trisail. But for coastal sailing it is important that the sail area be flexible enough to allow you to keep the boat moving, even in heavy weather.

The main objective when shortening down in heavy weather is to keep the boat balanced and make reasonable and safe headway. To balance the rig, you need to reduce the size of the sails fore and aft in roughly equal increments. The reason is twofold. First, a balanced rig will be the most efficient rig. Sailing with a headsail alone, as some sailors do, will give the boat a heavy lee helm that will make steering tiresome and will slow your headway. And, secondly, the sails themselves, even when reefed down, provide a shock-absorbing effect for the rig. As the boat pounds through the waves or falls off the face of the waves, the jarring to the rig can cause swagings and turnbuckles to fail. This is particularly true if the mainsail has been furled completely. It is far safer to keep small patches of sail aloft, on both the main and the headstay, to help the rig absorb the shock of high seas and jarring motions.

With that in mind, coastal sailing boats will be well advised to have both a small jib and a third reefing point in the mainsail. As conditions deteriorate, the headsails can be reduced while successive reefs are taken in the main. Although in boats with roller-reefing headsails the jib can be rolled in until only a scrap of sail is still catching the wind, you should remember to move the sheet lead car forward as the sail is reefed. Most skippers will not rig three sets of reefing lines in the mainsail for normal coastal sailing, for a second reef is usually sufficient. However, a third reefing line should be available and easily rigged in instances when the deepest reef is necessary.

Boats heading offshore should carefully analyze their need for short sails in an ocean storm. Most seasoned skippers will choose to carry proper storm sails and will know well in advance of needing to use them just how they are rigged and sheeted.

The storm trisail will spread approximately 30 percent of the mainsail area, but will be of higher aspect than the main and will be carried lower to the deck. The sail should be rigged on its own mast slide so the mainsail, once furled, will not have to be removed. The trisail does not sheet to the main boom, but will lead through snatch blocks rigged aft. When fitting out the boat with a trisail, it is important that the trisail leads are worked out and robust fittings installed to accept the snatch blocks.

Although more and more offshore boats sail with roller-reefing headsails, it is wise to carry a storm jib. Ideally, the storm jib will be rigged on a staysail stay well inboard of the headstay. In such an arrangement, the spitfire can be set to balance the trisail and will keep the boat balanced and moving through the water. If the storm jib is to be set on the headstay, it should be flown from a tack pennant to keep the foot of the sail well clear of any water breaking across the foredeck. The sheet leads for the storm jib or spitfire will be different from those for the normal working headsails. As was suggested for the trisail, when fitting out the boat for a storm jib, make sure appropriate deck hardware is in place to accept the sheets.

Once you have set your storm sails, the greatest risk to the sails and the rig will come from flogging and chafe. It is vital that robust sheets be used, for the strains of a strong wind on the sails, the sheets and the deck hardware will be enormous. A sheet badly led against a sharp object will chafe through in a matter of minutes. And, a sail left to flog for a few moments will destroy itself right before your eyes.

Although you may never need to use your storm sails, they represent solid insurance against the day when you find you no longer can carry your normal working sails.

HIGH SEAS BOAT HANDLING

The most important aspect of successful boat handling in storm conditions is to keep the boat and the sails under control at all times. The skipper and the helmsman will have to maintain constant vigilance to keep track of the sea state, the wind strength and how the boat and crew are coping with the situation.

In a gale or storm, most sailors will be amazed by the shriek of the wind. You will not be able to talk on deck in anything under a shout, and even shouting you have to be looking directly at the other person to be heard. The noise can be wearing and can be the cause of miscommunications, errors and poor decisions. It is important, then, to make certain you have heard clearly what has been said to you and, conversely, that you speak clearly and directly when you are giving instructions to the crew. Don't assume everyone has heard. Ask them if they understand.

Worse than the wind, however, are the waves. The sight of huge, black-faced breakers coming at you one after another and the feel of the boat as it lurches and strains under the pressure of the waves produce a unique and occasionally frightening experience. A breaker that chooses to break right on top of you can severely damage the boat, sweep away gear stowed on deck, a dodger or life lines, and can carry off crew members who are not secured with their harnesses.

Negotiating your way through high seas is the most serious and arduous task in storm sailing. While every boat will behave differently in these conditions, there are some general tactics that can make the ride easier and safer.

Sailing into the Storm

If your best and safest course is to windward, then you will have your sails trimmed in tightly, you will have the wind and spray in your eyes and you will be faced with the high seas coming at you. The key to sailing against large and occasionally breaking waves is to keep your speed moderate. If you are sailing too fast, particularly in a light, fairly flat-bottomed boat, you will find yourself leaping off the tops of the waves and falling with a crash into the troughs behind. The jarring of such a fall can do damage to the hull and can throw the rig out of alignment, causing the mast to break.

Yet if you are sailing too slowly into a high sea, you will find that in the troughs your sails can become blanketed by the wave and your forward motion will stop. You will lose steerage and will be unable to adjust your course to avoid a breaking crest.

Steering an oceangoing boat through a steep sea is an art. The basic tactic is to steer a series of S-shaped courses. As you come down the back of a wave, head off slightly to gain speed and control of the boat. Carry your speed into the trough and then, as the next wave approaches, head up slightly so you can take the wave on the bow. Once you have breasted the top of the wave, repeat the process.

Tacking in a strong breeze requires timing and precision. To avoid falling into irons, even briefly, you will want to time your tack to coincide with the moment you come over the top of a wave. Free the leeward sheet as the bow comes into the wind and then sheet it in again as quickly as possible while sailing down the back of the wave. It is important to keep your forward momentum and to avoid being caught by the next wave without enough speed to climb easily over the top of it.

The process of sailing to windward in bad weather can be complicated by several factors. If the low creating the storm is moving rapidly, the wind will tend to shift while the seas remain more or less constant. You will find in such conditions that one tack will be favored into the seas. If you have sea room and can afford to sail on the favored tack, you will find that the going will be easier for a while.

As soon, however, as the wind shifts, a new set of waves will begin to roll in over the old set, creating a confused sea boiling with

Sailing to windward in a gale requires concentration. To maintain boat speed, you have to maintain steerage. Steer slightly off the wind while in the trough, then head up directly into the wave as it passes so you meet the wave bow-on. Your course will be a continuous S-curve through the waves.

breakers. In such circumstances, the helmsman's job becomes particularly difficult. He must keep his eyes open and his hand on the wheel. As wave sets meet and break, he should be able to see how the patterns are forming and will be able to steer the boat to avoid sailing directly into a collision with a breaker.

Rogue waves at sea are rare, yet the conditions that will generate such waves can be found in waters where two large wave trains are meeting. You will see waves unlike normal storm waves and will on occasion witness the creation of a truly huge wave. If you are alert and can see the waves forming to windward of you, you may be able to maneuver the boat out of the path of one of the monsters.

Sailing Before the Wind

Without doubt, experienced sailors would choose to sail before a gale instead of into it. The ride is softer, the apparent wind is less, and the spray is on your back instead of in your eyes.

Yet sailing before the wind may be slightly more hazardous than into the wind. The problems to be overcome are twofold: speed and the ability to steer. The dangers to be avoided are being pooped, when green water comes over the stern; broaching sideways as you run down the face of a wave; and being pitch poled, when a breaking wave lifts your stern so high that the boat capsizes ass-over-teakettle.

Controlling your speed downwind requires the right amount of sail. Each boat responds differently to running in a storm. Lighter boats with high-lift keels and buoyant ends will be hard to steer and should set the storm sails well inboard—a storm jib on an inner forestay, for example—to keep the center of effort close to the center of lateral resistance. On heavier, full-keel boats, you may find that setting the storm jib on the headstay will help to keep the bow of the boat pointed downwind and thus the boat will be easier to sail.

Veteran ocean sailors each have a favorite approach to running in strong winds. But many find that broad reaching across the front of the waves and then making a turn down the face of the wave as it breaks—causing the boat to surge forward—gives the best control and the least chance for either a broach or a sideways rollover.

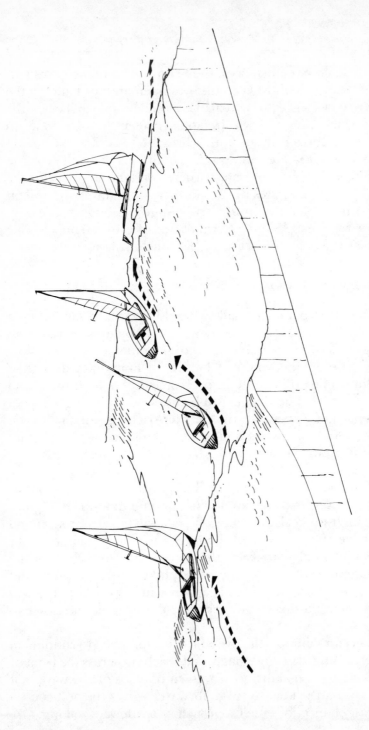

When steering downwind in high seas and a strong breeze, it is best to keep the wind on one quarter in order to avoid an accidental jibe and to prevent the boat from sailing too fast down the face of the wave. As a wave crest begins to build behind you and you can feel the stern lifting, head off and straight down the face of the wave, surfing if possible. This will help you avoid a broach which can lead to a rollover.

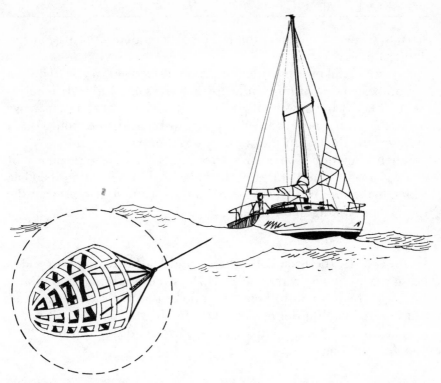

If you are surfing too fast as you run downwind before a gale, you run the risk of burying the bow in the wave ahead of you, which in turn can lead to being pooped or even pitchpoled. To slow the boat, stream anchor rodes, or a commercially available device such as the Gale Rider, from the stern.

If you have reduced sail to the minimum yet are still surging ahead too fast, you will find that you reach the bottom of the wave before it breaks. On occasion, you can even bury your bow in the backside of the wave ahead of you. This is a classic way to be pooped. And, if the breaking waves are large enough, you can get pitchpoled when running too fast.

Dragging warps over the stern is a proven way to apply the brakes and slow the boat. An anchor rode led in a loop from the stern cleats on either side of the transom should be played out. If the warp won't bite into the wave, you will have to stream an anchor or some other heavy object from the warp. Streaming warps will help hold your stern to the wind and will inhibit the boat's tendency to surge ahead and/or broach.

A commercial product that has proven effective as a way to put on the brakes when running in a storm is the Gale Rider. It is fabricated of heavy nylon webbing sewn into the shape of an open-weave basket. At its opening, a flexible plastic tube holds the mouth open and permits the Gale Rider to bite into the sea.

When streaming warps or a Gale Rider, be sure that plenty of chafe gear is applied at the stern chalks. And when using the Gale Rider, make sure you have a swivel in the towing line to prevent the rode from kinking and breaking.

IN HIGH SEAS, the least comfortable and least safe angle of sail is beam reaching across the waves. If the wind is strong enough and the waves high enough, being caught beam on by a breaker can cause a 90- or 100-degree knockdown. In the worst case, being caught full on by a breaking beam sea can send you and your boat on a full rollover.

HEAVING-TO

Heavy weather wears on a boat, tears on the sails and gradually takes a mighty toll on the crew. Exhaustion from lack of sleep, from worry and from the persistent roar of waves and wind can be blamed for more problems at sea than any other single cause. When you're too tired to sail on, when the crew is feeling battered and sick, when the boat seems to be overpowered, you will know it is time to stop for a while and heave-to.

There are conditions in which it is unwise and unsafe to heave-to. When waves are constantly breaking all around you, when you can feel the pounding of breakers on the deck and hull, you may be safer and happier to carry on running before the storm at a slow and controlled rate—possibly under bare poles with warps streamed astern.

However, in most storm conditions, heaving-to will be the option that presents itself when you feel you are done in and want to rest. In fact, after struggling to sail on in a storm, the act of heaving-to has an almost immediate positive effect upon the crew. The boat's motion eases, the fury of the wind seems to abate slightly, and the stress on gear, sails and the crew's morale seems to dissipate.

For cruising sailors, heaving-to need not be solely a storm tactic. Stopping the boat at any time, to navigate or make repairs or simply to have a quiet dinner, is an option too often overlooked. If you're not in a hurry, then stopping for a while can be a real pleasure.

But heaving-to is most often done when the wind is really piping. There are three generally accepted ways to heave-to in a sailboat: lying to a sea anchor or para-anchor; lying ahull; and heaving-to under reduced sail.

Lying to a Sea Anchor

The technology of sea anchors goes back to the last century, when fishermen developed sturdy canvas cones with iron hoops at the mouth for use when lying offshore in a storm. The sea anchors on the market today, most notably those designed and built by Dan Shewmon, are evolutions of the early canvas style. Relying on the conical shape to trap seawater, the anchor grips the water just under the surface and provides the drag needed to hold the bow of the boat to windward.

A traditional sea anchor needs to be quite large to hold the weight and windage of a larger, ocean-sailing boat. It should be attached to the boat with a long length of anchor rode and, like the Gale Rider, should be fitted with at least one swivel to prevent the rode from kinking. The rode should be well protected from chafe.

An alternative to the traditional sea anchor is the para-anchor, which is a huge, lightweight sea anchor designed along the lines of a parachute. Para-anchors are sewn of heavy nylon fabric and reinforced with nylon webbing. The anchor is usually set from the bow and, like a sea anchor, should be fitted with swivels and plenty of chafing gear.

Deploying a sea anchor or para-anchor can be difficult, for it will be caught and tossed about by the wind and will take some time to open and fill once in the water. The rode should be played out long enough to place the anchor two wave crests to windward of you and should be adjusted to account for changes in the wave patterns.

The danger in lying to a sea anchor or para-anchor is sliding backward as a breaking sea rolls under the bow of the boat. The hull slips back on the wave and the entire weight of the hull will fall onto the rudder. If the rudder turns as the boat goes astern, the pressure can easily bend the rudder post or shear off even the most robust pintels and gudgeons.

Experience will tell you quite quickly if the drift of the sea anchor and the size of the waves make lying to the anchor an unsafe proposition. In most seas and on most boats a sea anchor will be a useful storm tool. But it should be used with caution and a ready willingness to try another approach should backing on the rudder become a problem.

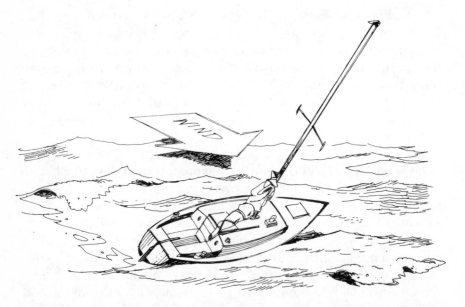

Lying to a sea anchor: When it is time to stop sailing, lying to a sea anchor can help you weather a gale. The sea anchor should be fitted with a swivel and should be made fast to the sturdiest point on deck. Beware of drifting backwards onto your rudder.

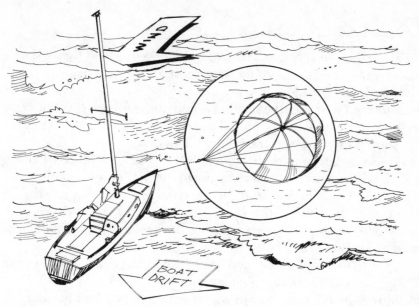

Lying ahull is the most passive way to deal with a gale. With all sails secured and the boat closed up, you simply let the boat find its own way among the waves. The main danger when lying ahull is being rolled by an unexpected breaker.

Lying Ahull

No storm tactic is more controversial than lying ahull. The technique is simply to douse all sail, batten down the boat and let it find its own natural position in the sea. The tiller is usually tied to leeward (wheel to windward) to help the boat keep her bow from falling off too far. The natural windage of the rig and the bow will normally force the bow away from the wind, while the rudder tends to force the bow back again.

Heavier cruising boats with full keels will be extremely sluggish lying ahull and will tend to find a position approximately beam-on to the seas. In this position, the boat will roll to each new wave while moving ahead slowly and making a lot of leeway. It can be an uncomfortable angle, yet if the boat settles down, this can be a restful way to weather a storm.

In lighter boats, with little wetted surface and light, high, buoyant ends, the bow will tend to fall off slightly beyond the beam reach to approximately 100 to 135 degrees from the wind. Waves will tend to break on the windward quarter and will shove the boat forward with each crest while also pivoting the bow slightly to windward.

In both types of boat, the pressure of the waves and wind will be transformed first into the healing angle of the boat and second into leeway. In seas that are not breaking ferociously, lying ahull may be the simplest way to stop the boat while you rest.

However, the danger in lying ahull is the possibility of being rolled. As the boat makes leeway down the face of a breaking wave, the keel will tend to drag and the force of the wind will push the rig to leeward, increasing the boat's angle of heel. Should the wave break onto the boat, further rotating the keel to windward and the mast to leeward, you could face a complete rollover.

Other than being pitchpoled, there is nothing more dangerous in a big sea than a rollover. The rig will be carried away. Deck gear, including the life raft, may be swept off the boat. And in modern, beamy cruisers with low stability angles, there is the distinct possibility of remaining upside down as the boat stabilizes in an inverted position.

Lying ahull has its proponents. Yet, if the seas are large and breaking, you may be wise to choose another tactic for stopping the boat.

Heaving-To Under Reduced Sail

Although not the simplest way to stop the boat in heavy weather, heaving-to under reduced sail offers what many offshore sailors consider the best compromise in winds up to 50 knots. The need to control the speed of the boat while at the same time keeping adequate steerage makes many offshore sailors suspicious of either lying ahull or lying to a sea anchor. Heaving-to under deeply reduced sail can achieve both ends.

Each different design will show unique behavior in strong winds. It is essential to try out the various methods in a fresh breeze when you can judge best how your boat will behave and what combination of sails will perform best for you.

In modern masthead sloops of moderate to light displacement, the most common method of heaving-to in heavy weather is under storm jib alone. To heave-to, trim the storm jib to windward, force the bow off the wind and then tie the helm down to counteract the leeward force of the jib. The boat will seek a position approximately 60 degrees off the wind and will then proceed forward at one or two knots. The course will be erratic as the boat rides over large swells and falls off again in the gusts at the top of the wave. And the boat will occasionally take a breaking wave on the forward windward quarter that will shove the hull to leeward. Your progress under the storm jib alone will be a diagonal vector at about 130 degrees from the true direction of the wind, as you will be going forward at about two knots and going sideways at about one knot.

If the boat does not want to lie under storm jib alone, if it tends to

Heaving-to under reduced sail: With a storm trisail and a storm jib set, you can stop the boat and ease the noise and motion of hammering into a gale by heaving-to. Sheet the jib to windward and as flat as you can. Sheet the trisail to leeward, as flat as possible. Lash the rudder to leeward. The boat will jog forward at a knot or so and will behave quietly and easily. This is the preferred method of stopping in heavy weather.

have too much lee helm and can not approach the wave on a close reaching angle, you will want to add a bit of sail area aft. In a split-rigged boat, a ketch or a yawl, a deep reefed mizzen may do the trick. Or, in a sloop, you can fly the storm trisail, sheeted very flat. When adding sail in strong winds, do so advisedly and with great care. The strain on deck gear or the force of extreme gusts—over 60 knots or more—may mitigate against adding sail. However, it is important to remember that carrying a small main—a trisail or a triple reefed mainsail—with the storm jib will give additional support to the mainmast and the standing rigging.

Another tactic for heaving-to under reduced sail is under triple-reefed main alone. In winds under 50 knots, you may find that the boat balances better without a storm jib and will jog along sedately with the helm lashed amidships or slightly to weather with just the reduced main flying. The sail should be sheeted as flat as possible, with the traveler to leeward and the vang cranked down. If you have an adjustable backstay you will want to crank it down to more than half of its tightest setting, but do not crank it all the way down. A small amount of flexibility and play in the rig can save it from a stress failure.

It is important when heaving-to under the mainsail, triple reefed, to make certain that the sail is well tied down, that the halyard is strong enough to withstand the pumping it will receive from the sail, and that the main sheet and traveler are up to the job. You will have to monitor carefully the angle at which you lie to the wind and the stresses on the sail, the running rigging and the standing rigging to assess whether the forces of the wind are too great for the sail configuration.

In split-rigged boats, yawls and ketches, it is possible to heave-to under storm jib and mizzen as described above. Yet if the wind is too great for this combination, if the boat seems overpowered and labors in every gust, you may choose to drop the jib and heave-to under a deeply reefed mizzen alone. The sail should be sheeted hard amidships with the tiller to windward (or wheel to leeward), where they will act together to keep the bow off the wind at about 40 to 50 degrees. If your angle to the wind is too close, if blue water is coming over the bow, sheet the mizzen to leeward with a second sheet and adjust the helm farther to windward to force the bow down.

On a split-rigged boat such as a yawl or ketch, you can heave-to under the double-reefed mizzen and the backed storm jib.

Heaving-to under reduced sail will require more sail handling and helm maintenance than the other methods. Yet with some scraps of sail flying, you will find that you are able to adjust your speed to suit the conditions, and you will be able to hold steerage even through breaking seas. Finally, should you decide that the time has come to try a different course of action, you will have the maneuverability and the boat speed to change course.

THE SURVIVAL STORM

Few sailors have ever experienced a true survival storm at sea. How you make the gradation between a storm of 40 or 50 knots and a survival storm may well be a subjective evaluation of the conditions you find. Generally, sustained winds over 60 knots, with gusts higher, will create conditions that most sailors will consider a matter of life and death.

No text on sailing and safety can prescribe the best procedures to follow in such conditions, except to say that, given a choice, a safe harbor and robust anchor tackle will be much preferred to the fury of a survival storm in the open sea.

In a fully found, well-designed ocean-sailing vessel, you may be able to heave-to under reduced sail right through survival conditions. A good sea boat should put its shoulder down in such conditions and fiercely chew to windward, riding through and over the coming waves. But for the boat to do that, it will most likely have to be long and narrow, deep and heavy.

That is not the description of most of the boats in which we go to sea. Most are light, beamy and carry a shallow draft. They are not designed to survive a Force 12 storm. They are designed to cruise comfortably in a wide range of moderate conditions. How such a

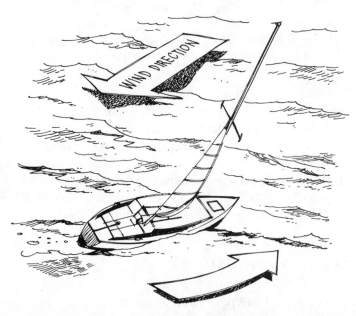

In a moderate gale or in instances when you do not have storm canvas, it is possible to heave-to under the triple-reefed mainsail. The sail should be reefed as flat as possible and then sheeted slightly to leeward. The tiller will have to be lashed slightly to windward, although you will have to find the right position for your own boat.

boat will react to the ravages of hurricane-force winds will depend
to a large extent upon its ability to be steered firmly and surely by a
large and robust rudder, by the strength of the rig, by its tendency
to recover from a dramatic roll—110 degrees at least—and by the
integrity of the hatches, ports and hull.

Naturally, the boat in a survival situation will behave at its best.
The crew, on the other hand, will usually prove to be the weak link.
How you prepare a crew for such conditions will be a matter of
personal resolve. There is no way to inject ultimate endurance into a
person of small heart, no way to instill a brute stubbornness to live
in the equivocal. In a survival storm, each member of the crew will
either have what it takes or he won't. A savvy skipper and savvy crew
will be able to sense the difference before leaving the dock.

Sailing tactics in a survival storm will depend upon the boat in
which you are sailing. If the boat is able to hold its own under storm
canvas, that will more than likely be the best course of action.
Progress will be slow, leeway will be great and your position will not
change dramatically over a period of hours. The crew will be able to
keep short watches, tend to maintenance below, watch for chafe on
deck and keep an eye on the barometer to see when the deepest
isobar finally swings past.

If your boat withers before a survival sea, as most will, then the
safest option is to head off and run under bare poles before the
wind and sea. Controlling speed will be critical. Three to five knots
through the water should be the range you shoot for, even though
you will accelerate alarmingly down the face of the storm seas.

Streaming warps or the Gale Rider will help you apply the brakes
and will help to keep the stern from slewing off sideways and
forcing a broach.

Those who have steered through such conditions often report
that the favored angle down the face of a huge wave is a wide, broad
reach, keeping the breaking crest on your windward quarter.
Should the crest begin to rise over you, you can head down and
surge before it toward the bottom of the trough, keeping fingers
crossed that it will not poop you or pitchpole you. How long you can
continue to steer before the wind will depend upon the strength of
the crew, for in such conditions 30 minutes at the helm will be
exhausting. If ever a well-prepared boat, with hot food in the ther-

mos, and a dry, orderly cabin below is a necessity, it is during such conditions.

Yet no matter how prepared you and your boat are for a survival storm, you will be reduced before the force of the wind and only determination and reservoirs of strength will see you through. And then you'll have a story to tell.

Chapter 9

ABANDON SHIP

The Choice: Active or Passive?
The Abandon-Ship Kit
Abandon-Ship Procedures
Survival

THERE IS NO telling when or why you might find yourself in a situation in which the integrity of your boat is so seriously compromised that you must prepare and execute an abandon-ship plan. The oceans of the world today carry an enormous amount of commercial traffic, so collisions at sea are a possible threat.

Container ships laden high with steel containers ply all of the world's seas and oceans; in bad weather, those containers are occasionally jettisoned or simply lost. There is no count of how many containers are lost at sea in any given year; underwriters, shipping companies and shipowners will not reveal the loss. Yet international convention limits the financial responsibility of the shipowner to a paltry $125 (U.S.) per lost container. In a bad sea it is in the ship captain's interest to dump his cargo. But his action litters the sea with lethal weapons that can sink an ocean-sailing boat in seconds.

Faulty sea cocks, a collision with a whale, a damaged rudder post and through-hull—these are all emergencies aboard that can lead to uncontrollable flooding.

It is in anticipation of such an emergency that prudent offshore sailors carry a spare boat, usually a life raft, and prepare themselves and their crew for the possibility—however remote—of having to put that lifesaving equipment to work. The thought of sinking and losing a valuable and much-loved boat is so hard to grapple with that many offshore skippers do not address the problem with their crew at all. Yet failing to integrate abandon-ship procedures into the overall crew briefing before setting off to sea is as thoughtless and irresponsible as failing to instruct the crew in the use of the head.

There are plenty of offshore sailors who take to long-passage-making without a raft, without a serious abandon-ship plan, without an EPIRB and with their fates securely wedded to their boats' integrity . . . and to good fortune.

But sound seamanship, experience and prudence dictate that a skipper who is planning to make miles offshore for a far-flung coast, whether a few hundred miles or a few thousand, should carry a spare boat—a life raft—and should be prepared and equipped to

Cruising World/Susan Waterman

In the unlikely event of having to abandon ship, make certain the crew is well prepared and that the lifesaving equipment is handy and up to the job.

use it in a seamanlike fashion. The expense of a raft is high. You can expect to pay $2,000 or more for a suitable and safe raft. The expense of an abandon-ship kit is also high. You will have to spend more than $1,000 to fill a smallish bag with the essentials for survival in a raft.

It's insurance.

No skipper ever expects to use his raft and the gear he has assembled for survival in the spare boat. But the plain responsibility of being the skipper, of being the owner and master of a boat headed off across open water, requires that he provide a last-ditch emergency option for his crew.

THE CHOICE: ACTIVE OR PASSIVE?

The debate about the best way to anticipate and prepare for an abandon-ship emergency has gone on for decades. Although an inflatable life raft may seem at first look to be the spare boat of choice for offshore sailors, that is not the case. There are some among the community of ocean sailors who have decided that there is another, better route.

At the heart of the debate is the question: Should a crew in dire straits abandon their own self-reliance and place themselves in a rescue pod in which they can await outside help? Or should a castaway crew, faced with the loss of their mother ship, take to their spare boat and continue on under their own power and guided by their own initiative toward a safe harbor?

It is a provocative question, one not easily answered.

Those who choose the passive route are the majority. The solution to an abandon-ship emergency is to carry aboard an inflatable spare boat—a life raft—in which the crew will huddle, stationary, as they await the assistance of rescuers. In this case, the survival plan depends on the effectiveness of the worldwide rescue system—Amvers or associated programs—and on the ability of the crew to wait, passively and healthily, for help to arrive.

One of the assumptions of the passive plan is that the seas are high, so that negotiating any small spare boat will be hazardous and foolhardy. One should evacuate the sunken mother ship and sit in the life raft while the electronic beepers—the EPIRB and the radio calls—bring help.

In fact, the passive approach, which depends on the good wishes of commercial shipping, commercial aircraft and on the navies and coastal patrols of the world, is a sound approach. The rescue mechanism—the radio signals, the aircraft, the military and the commercial traffic—is all in place. It is, by the conventions of the sea, waiting for your call. Should you make the call from the damp, cold confines of a raft with the EPIRB, they will, ostensibly, come running.

On the other side of the question is a different perspective. Those who champion this cause are the fiercely self-reliant. They swallow one bittersweet pill—they have gone to sea of their own accord, they are seafaring for pleasure and thus deserve no assistance from commercial and military craft. This point of view dictates that an abandon-ship emergency be met with a spare boat that will carry the crew home to a safe harbor. The boat will, most likely, be a dinghy, rigged with a canopy, oars and a sailing rig.

The assumption of the active approach is that no matter what the conditions, no amateur sailor who has put his life at risk for pleasure should have the gall to call professionals for help. Moreover, the assumption is that most emergency sinkings—striking a container, a whale, a tree stump—will occur in conditions in which it is possible to handle a small spare boat.

The choice of which route to take will depend upon the skipper's own personal attitude. Yet, whichever choice you make, the job of preparing for an abandon-ship emergency does not end with the acquisition of a life raft or an unsinkable dinghy. Both need to be fitted out for the task they may have to perform and both should be fitted out with the gear you will need to protect you from the elements, feed yourself and signal for help.

THE ABANDON-SHIP KIT

A certain amount of gear will be stored in a high-quality commercial life raft. Depending upon the manufacturer and the options available, you will be provided with several cans of distilled water, packages of food, flares, space blankets, a small medical kit, a flashlight, fishing gear and an EPIRB. But this list is only the beginning.

No matter where you are when forced to abandon the mother ship—unless in an enclosed bay—you must plan for survival in the raft for an indefinite period. To do so you will have to supplement the equipment supplied in the raft with an abandon-ship kit. The kit bag itself should be waterproof and buoyant. Bags built for dinghy racing, canoeing and river rafting can all be suitable to the purpose. It helps if the bag is a bright color and can be fitted with a long polypropylene line.

The abandon-ship kit will be the key to surviving a long period adrift in a raft. It must contain the essentials for staying alive and should be customized to suit the needs of the crew. Once filled, the bag should not be tucked away at the bottom of a sail locker. It should be accessible and easily brought on deck.

Water

The first requirement for surviving as a castaway is fresh water. While there have been cases of sailors in rafts surviving for long periods by sipping small amounts of seawater, the practice should not be encouraged. Fresh water is what the body requires, so fresh water is what you should be prepared to provide. Have at least one, preferably two, five-gallon jerry jugs tied on deck for emergency use. The jugs should not be filled completely, so that they will float if tossed into the water.

Solar stills, such as the still developed during World War II for British flyers, are available through some chandleries or catalogs. A simple solar still will make between two and four cups of fresh water a day.

A better but more expensive option is a reverse-osmosis desalinator that can be operated by hand. One such device, built by Recovery Engineering, provided fresh water for Simonne and William Butler during their 66 days adrift in the Pacific after their boat was sunk by whales in 1989. Needless to say, the Butlers were enthusiastic about the water maker. If you splurge on any item for the

Cruising World/Susan Waterman

The life raft will contain the basics for a short survival period. It should be augmented with a well-fitted-out survival kit stowed near the raft.

abandon-ship kit, such a water maker—costing $500 or more— may well be the item to choose.

Lastly, a simple, manually operated juice press will help you squeeze drops of moisture from the flesh of fish or other sea life. Although bulky, a juicer might provide enough liquid to save your life. If you choose to carry one, make sure it is made of stainless steel.

Exposure

Once you have taken to a life raft, the greatest risk to your well-being, after dehydration, is exposure. A raft is surrounded by water and exposed to wind and sun. Most rafts have canopies and better rafts have inflated double floors to insulate you from the elements. Also, a raft is prone to fill with water, so you will always be sitting or lying on a wet surface.

To combat the effects of the elements and to protect yourself from hypothermia and the ravages of exposure, your survival kit should include several space blankets in which to wrap yourself. Additionally, polypropylene long underwear can be packed for each crew member. Polypropylene wicks moisture away from the skin and can be dried with a vigorous shake. The fabric is comfortable, will not rot when wet and will keep your skin in better condition than any other cloth.

Another preventive measure against the damage caused by exposure is zinc ointment. Pack several tubes of zinc cream to apply to the faces of the crew to prevent sun damage. More importantly, zinc ointment will help alleviate the sores on legs and backsides which can be so debilitating.

If you are sailing in cold waters, you should prepare yourself with a raft that has a double floor. In addition, if you know you will be in a cold climate, you may wish to require each crew member to bring his own survival suit. Although expensive and bulky, a survival suit will preserve body heat, will keep moisture out and will prevent chafing of your skin.

Lastly, raising your body temperature when the elements around you are well below 98.6 degrees is a difficult task. It is wise, if you are sailing in temperate or cool climates, to pack a good supply of chemical heat pouches, available at most camping and mountaineering stores.

Food

In the inflated raft, you will find supplies that might last a crew for a few days. This will be enough to get you started, but you will need more if you find yourself adrift in waters that are far from shore and off the beaten track. In your abandon-ship kit you should not only keep stored a good supply of food—such as raisins, granola bars, high-protein bars and other concentrated foods—but you should have the gear you will need to forage from the sea.

No matter where you are at sea, there will be something to eat. The waters of the world are filled with life; you just have to be able to catch it. Moreover, a drifting raft has a way of becoming a haven for plant and fish life. In a matter of days a raft will begin to sprout slimy growths. In a week or two, weeds and barnacles will be growing. Over several weeks, you will find that the bottom of the raft has evolved a complex and fecund environment of plants, crustaceans and fish.

It is the fish you are after. Fish will appear in the shadow of the raft soon after you become a castaway. To catch them you will need some basic equipment. In the raft you will most likely find fish-hooks, a roll of monofilament line and possibly a knife. To this you can add a few important items.

A short spear gun will catch you more food than any other weapon. You can purchase a short-barrel spear gun from some dive shops, or you can fashion your own. It is important that the shaft be firmly attached to the gun with a sturdy lanyard. And the point must be sheathed or have a cork or rubber tip to prevent it from tearing the raft.

Lures may not be provided in the raft's fishing kit. In the abandon-ship kit, store a small box of spinning lures and feather lures. You will also want to store a roll of monofilament line, spare hooks and a pair of cheap gardening gloves. The gloves will prevent water-softened hands from being cut by the fishing line and will make cleaning spiny fish or sea turtles less dangerous.

A small plankton net should be included in the fishing box. The net will be a source of bait for fishing and, in a pinch, can provide a small amount of raw protein for you to eat.

Medical Kit

In most rafts, a small medical kit will be provided by the manufac-turer or retailer. However, this will be sufficient for only the most common medical problems you are likely to face in a raft. In it you will find bandages, antiseptic and antibacterial creams, seasick pills and possibly finger splints and tape.

You will want to pack your own additional materials, which will include any medications you require, painkillers in varying strengths, a general antibiotic such as tetracycline, burn ointment for sun lesions, eyewash, more bandages, rolls of surgical tape and scissors.

Unless you are a doctor or are sailing with a doctor, it is unwise to think that you will be able to deal with serious medical emergencies in a raft. Do not overburden your emergency medical kit with a wide range of treatments. Yet you will want to provide treatments for such easily anticipated ailments as seasickness, sunburn, small cuts, infections, internal infections and diarrhea.

Communications

Once in a raft, your primary concern is not to drift to safety but to alert possible rescuers to your plight. At the onset of an abandon-ship emergency, you should set off your EPIRB and send a Mayday call via the radio.

The gear you carry in your abandon-ship kit with which to communicate with rescuers should be as comprehensive as possible. Visual distress signals will be packed into the raft, typically three or four hand-held flares and two or three rocket or parachute flares.

In addition to these, you will want to add at least four SOLAS-approved parachute flares and four SOLAS-approved hand-held flares. These are expensive at approximately $100 apiece. Yet if you

Cruising World/Susan Waterman

The emergency position-indicating beacon—EPIRB—can be the best link between you and those trying to rescue you.

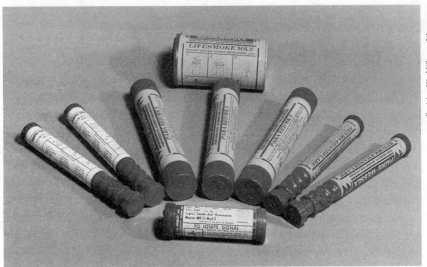

A good supply of flares is a must. SOLAS-approved quality is worth the extra money the flares will cost.

can afford more and have room in your kit bag, carry more. You can almost be assured you will not be seen by a passing freighter, no matter how many flares you fire at him.

A waterproof flashlight is a useful tool. It will give you light in the raft after darkness falls and can be used to train a beam of light onto the bridge of a ship or at a low-flying aircraft. The flashlight should have fresh batteries and a button for sending a Morse SOS.

A signaling mirror is an inexpensive and extremely powerful tool for sending a flashing distress signal. In bright sunlight, the reflection off a mirror can be seen for many miles and is unmistakable. Inexpensive, durable and requiring no maintenance, a signaling mirror is an essential item.

A dye marker is a useful communication tool if you have been able to get off a Mayday signal on your ship's radio and know that there will be a plane or ships out looking for you. If a rescue is in full swing, then deploy the dye marker in a slow, judicious way, leaving a series of large stains on the ocean surface. But if you doubt a rescue operation is under way, the dye marker will be wasted in the open sea.

A noisemaker of some type should be carried. A loud metal whistle may be the best option, for it is small, inexpensive and will create a loud enough noise to be heard over the din of a ship's engines. Other sound makers, such as a freon horn or a pistol, will help to get a rescuer's attention as well, but will be harder to stow in a kit bag and will require a lot of maintenance.

The last item for communications that should be put into the abandon-ship bag is a hand-held VHF radio. Old salts will think of a hand-held radio as a needless luxury. But in the modern world of seafaring, every ship, boat or plane that is crossing open water is equipped with VHF and uses it frequently. A hand-held VHF will enable you to shout at a passing freighter that has failed to see your flares, failed to see your mirror signals, failed to notice the dye marker and turned a deaf ear to your whistles or pistol shots. Every commercial vessel is required to monitor Channel 16 while under way. They don't all do so, particularly commercial fishing fleets. Yet they are all monitoring some frequency and a synthesized hand-held VHF with spare batteries will be able to get through if you have a lot of patience and a little luck.

Navigational Materials

It will be useful to have in the raft a small-scale chart of the body of water you are sailing in. The chart will give you a way to monitor your progress as you drift with surface currents and will give you information on shipping routes in your area. A journal or log is useful, so you can keep track of weather, sightings of ships, your position and your thoughts. A small hand-held compass—such as a simple Boy Scout compass—will help you determine your drift and will give you bearings on any land you might see. And, don't forget pencils and a pencil sharpener. All of this will fit neatly into a small plastic valise, which should have a watertight closure—such as a large, heavy-duty Ziploc bag.

THE ABANDON-SHIP KIT is your own personal piece of survival luggage. You will have to equip it as best you can and maintain it at regular intervals during the normal course of the year, while remembering that in its contents lies the possible fate of all who sail with you.

ABANDON-SHIP PROCEDURES

If you have been sailing in heavy weather prior to finding yourself in an abandon-ship emergency, you will probably have put in place an onboard duty roster, allocating tasks to the crew. Such a duty roster was discussed in Chapter 8.

The purpose of the duty roster is to make certain that what needs to be done in the minutes you have before an evacuation, is done. There will be confusion, but the order of business should be clear enough for everyone on board to have a good idea of what he is supposed to do.

The decision to leave the mother ship for the spare boat will be made by the skipper. As soon as the decision is reached, the skipper should announce the plan to the crew and repeat clearly the tasks each must perform.

If all the members of the crew are not wearing their safety harness and life preserver at this point, they should immediately put them on. The life jacket should be equipped with a light and a whistle. As you leave the boat and take to the raft, there is a better than even chance that one or all of the crew will end up in the water, with the potential of being separated from the raft by wind and waves.

Launching the Raft

The crew member who has been responsible for maintaining order on deck, for checking rigging and setting up jacklines, should be put in charge of the raft. He should have a rigging knife on his belt or readily available. The raft should be tied to the boat with its supplied painter. The painter will be 20 to 40 feet long and will need to be pulled completely from the raft container to kick off inflation. Don't make the mistake of throwing the raft overboard before pulling out most of the painter. The raft should be launched amidships on the leeward side. Yank the painter sharply and continue to pull until the inflated raft is close to the boat.

The raft should inflate right side up. If it has an inflatable canopy, the canopy will turn it over should it inflate upside down. But if the raft does not have a canopy, or has a canopy that has to be inflated manually, you may have to flip the raft while you are still on the deck of the boat.

It will take a minute or more for the raft to inflate and, once inflated, it will take another minute or so for the ballast bags to fill completely and stabilize the platform.

Be wary of sharp objects on the side and decks of the boat, such as sail tracks, broken stanchions, cotter pins and other deck gear. You don't want to tear the raft's fabric before you get a chance to get into it.

If you have an unsinkable dinghy on deck or astern, or wind surfers and surf boards, these should be launched as well and tied to the raft.

Your spare boats are now ready. The rest of the crew will be performing other chores. If possible, the crew member who launched the raft and the other boats should tend them to prevent them from crashing against the boat or, worse, drifting away.

The Navigator

Knowing where you are precisely and letting others know your position should be the prime responsibilities of the navigator. As you realize that you are getting into trouble, it is important to fix your position as accurately as possible. Make sure you write out your latitude and longitude on a piece of paper and figure the position to seconds of arc if possible. This position should be backed up with other information available, such as loran coordinates, depth readings, RDF bearings or radar bearings.

Once this information has been assembled, the decision will be made to transmit a Mayday call. If you have a long-range radio—SSB or ham—make contact with a shore station and transmit your exact position three times. Include the name of your boat, the color of your boat and raft and the number of crew and ask for a reply.

If you do not have long-range radio, try making the Mayday call on Channel 16, even if there is no ship traffic in the vicinity. Follow the procedure above, making sure you repeat your position three times, at the least. If you do not receive a reply, you won't know if you have made contact or not. Your hope will be that the signal has found a ship or an aircraft that is unable to get its signal back to you.

Once the Mayday has been sent, the navigator should set off the EPIRB and make sure it is transmitting. The EPIRB, if functioning, will broadcast an emergency signal to overflying aircraft, to shipping and to satellites. In the absence of a voice radio contact, the EPIRB signal is your last radio link. It must come with you into the life raft.

The navigator should be in charge of getting the abandon-ship kit on deck and ready to go into the raft. A lanyard should be tied to the bag to prevent it from becoming lost in the confusion of trying to board the raft.

The Galley Crew

If time allows, the person who has been in charge of the galley during the heavy weather should do his utmost to collect food and liquids to supplement the gear in the raft and in the abandon-ship kit. Use a sail bag or duffel bag and toss into it small water jugs, crackers, cans, peanut butter and whatever else you can get your hands on. If you bring cans, also bring a can opener. There should be one in the raft. A spare is reassuring. Sponges will be useful in the raft, so toss in any lying about the galley.

Once the food and drink has been assembled, the galley crew member should take it on deck and prepare it for transfer to the life raft. A lanyard should be tied to the bag.

The second and possibly most vital job for the galley crew member is to unlash the deck water jugs, tie lanyards on them and prepare them for the raft.

Getting into the Raft

Depending on the sea state, the strength of the wind, the condition of the mother ship and the organization of the crew, getting into the raft can be either a simple transfer or a nightmare.

In rough conditions, the strongest crew member should attempt to bring the raft alongside the boat while another climbs aboard.

Launching a life raft: (1) The raft should be readied on the leeward side of the boat. (2) The raft's attaching line should be pulled from the cannister until slight resistance is met. (3) The raft should be launched close to the boat and inflated quickly. (4) Once inflated, tie the raft close to the boat so it does not blow away. (5) If the raft inflated inverted, you should right it as soon as possible.

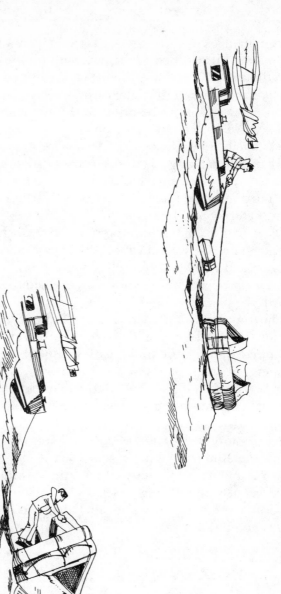

This maneuver may require the boarding crew member to get into the water while clipped to the boat with his life harness. Once he is into the raft, the harness should be unclipped from the boat and immediately made fast to the raft.

Once a person is in the raft, throw him the lanyards for the bags and gear you will be bringing aboard and then begin to pass them across one by one. If possible, do not throw gear, for the wind will carry it away, making the transfer more difficult. You may, however, have to drop water jugs into the sea so the man in the raft can pull them in and heave them aboard. Make certain the water jugs have tight, waterproof screw tops.

Once gear is loaded into the raft, the crew should leave the boat one at a time. Each should attach his safety harness to the painter of the raft and then pull himself along the line until he reaches the raft. Once the last crew member has reached the raft and is safely on board, the painter should be cut.

The importance of having a sharp knife at hand ready to cut the painter cannot be stressed too much. Better life rafts will come equipped with a knife in a sheath mounted next to the end of the painter. But you should also have your own.

In high seas and a gale wind, the painter will become tangled in the boat's rigging as it goes down. Safety harnesses also can become tangled. In the fury and confusion of the last few seconds of an abandon-ship emergency, people will forget how to untie simple knots, they will leave lines attached when they should be free, and they will do helpful things that bind the raft to the sinking boat. A knife will be your only way to separate yourself from the foundering vessel and its flailing rig and avoid damaging collisions with the boat as it is going down.

LEAVING A SINKING boat, one that you have prepared and in which you have invested countless hours, dollars and dreams, may be the most difficult decision a sailor ever faces. The harsh reality of the decision, of the situation, of the loss, comes home with a fierce crunch in the moments after the crew has taken to the raft. The sinking boat, broken and disabled, begins to founder as waves break over it. The mast tilts oddly. The cabin disappears and then in a long whoosh, the boat is gone. All around is the blank sea, and nothing else.

SURVIVAL

In most cases of crews cast away to the tenuous rubber confines of a life raft, rescuers are on the scene in a matter of hours or days. The Mayday has been heard, the EPIRB signal has been received and the worldwide mechanism of search and rescue at sea has begun to whir with its amazing efficiency.

Yet, in the hours following the sinking of the mother ship, there is no way to know when help will arrive or even if it will arrive. The ordeal may go on only a few more hours or it may go on for tens of days. How the crew responds to that uncertainty will decide how well you survive for whatever length of time you must wait in the raft for help.

In case after case, those who have been responsible for the boat, the skipper or owner, have shown deep depression in the days following the disaster. Not only is the loss of the ship a shattering experience, but the sense of failure can be devastating. A skipper always feels responsible for the safety and well-being of his crew. Losing the mother ship and putting the crew in the highly unsafe and possibly lethal predicament of surviving in a life raft can be an experience that causes derangement, delusions and outright madness.

In a few recorded instances, the skippers of lost ocean-sailing boats have faded quickly once in their life rafts and have finally lost control of themselves and the situation and swum away to lose themselves in the waves. The psychological problems to be overcome in a life raft are as demanding and important as the more basic problems of water, food and survival.

Surviving in a life raft requires a fierce determination to live and a willingness to improvise solutions to just about any basic human problem. In such circumstances, it is vital that all members of the

crew—husbands and wives, old friends, hired hands, whomever—
know that their own survival depends upon the survival of the
whole crew.

If the skipper is able, he must remain in command. But his rule
over the tiny confines of the life raft must be dedicated to the
survival of the group and not just himself and his favorites. If the
skipper is disabled, physically or psychologically, then another in
the crew must assume a leadership role. The spirit of the raft must
always be one of indomitability. The person in the raft who feels this
most deeply will bear the burden of infecting others with the spirit.

There are many tales told of survival in rafts and some lessons to
be learned. It is possible to catch enough fish to live. In most areas
there will be sufficient rain to replenish the drinking supply, if water
is managed very carefully. People will get sick, they will get sores,
and they will suffer from exposure and hypothermia. All in the raft
must work together to alleviate these problems.

The importance of routine and of crew participation cannot be
overly stressed. No one person can bear the entire weight of managing the situation. A skipper must delegate chores and duties; not
because there is so much that must be done, but because people who
are actively participating in their own survival will carry on long
after passive souls have withered.

The raft's leader must establish a routine as soon as possible. It
will help to have duties written down and given daily review. There
should be someone in charge of the water, someone who takes on the
responsibility of medical officer, someone who coordinates the
watch system and someone who looks after signaling equipment
and radios.

If all trapped in the raft are working together in the spirit of
cooperation, they will each add strength to the others and vastly
increase the chance of rescue and survival.

Chapter 10

THE SKIPPER'S RESPONSIBILITY

The "Old Man": Captain Bligh or Captain
  Cook?
The Skipper as Manager
Decision Making Aboard a Boat
The Art of Delegation
A Crew's Bill of Rights
Conclusion

NEARLY 20 YEARS AGO I had the good fortune to sail into Tahiti
after a pleasant and leisurely crossing of the Pacific from Panama.
The trade wind passage from Central America via the Galapagos,
Marquesas and Tuamotus was a happy one. I was aboard a vin-
tage Tahiti ketch belonging to John Kiley, now a naval architect in
Boston. The voyage was made all the better by our skipper's complete competence, knowledge, forethought and seamanship—even
though he was only 23 at the time.

So it was with a real sense of surprise that in Tahiti I witnessed

The waterfront in Papeete, Tahiti, is one of the legendary landfalls sought by cruising sailors. It is also one of the spots where inexperienced or incompetent skippers lose their crews, as Captain Bligh did when he sailed in aboard the HMS *Bounty*.

time and again the obverse of that experience. While we were moored stern-to-the-quay in Papeete, boat after boat arrived only to have one or more of the crew standing on deck with bags packed. The last stern line would be made fast to a bollard, the dinghy would go over the side, and the impatient crew would be in it and ashore as quickly as possible. Something aboard was not right, and the crew—too often a wife or girlfriend—was doing something immediate about it.

As we got to know the cruising people along the quay, those who sailed happily together and those who did not, one thing became clear: Well-run boats kept their crews. Boats run poorly lost them. Moreover, well-skippered boats had few incidents of breakdown, few accidents, few horror stories and few disasters. Boats run poorly had more than their share of sea tales to relate over Hinanos at the quayside bars.

The difference between pleasant, safe sailing and unpleasant, unsafe sailing lay squarely in the conduct of the skipper.

When you consider the wide range of knowledge a competent skipper must command—from engine maintenance to navigation to coping with authorities and much more—it's a wonder that there are not more stories of mishap and loss at sea. In fact, coastal and offshore sailing is generally a safe experience for all involved. Statistically, it is more dangerous to drive your car from your home to the marina than it is to sail across an ocean. That's not because sailing is inherently less dangerous than driving. It is because sailing is an acquired pastime that carries with it a heavy weight of tradition, shared experience and accepted behavior.

Additionally, sailing requires a high degree of self-reliance. Any newcomer to coastal cruising soon learns that he must rely on his own competence to be successful. Knowing that breeds forethought, study, preparation and safe practices in most cases.

Yet, amidst all of the traditions of the sea which help to guide a sailor to a safer and more pleasant time on the water, the role of the skipper remains paramount. A skipper who does his homework diligently and then executes the command of his little ship with care will cruise successfully the world around. Those who don't, end their sailing experiences with tales of woe—tales that commonly blame the crew for the skipper's own incompetence.

THE "OLD MAN": CAPTAIN BLIGH OR CAPTAIN COOK?

Being the master of a ship—large or small—is an awesome responsibility. A skipper invites others to sail with him for pleasure and adventure. He puts to sea and thereby puts both the boat and the crew at some risk. The care of the ship is his ultimate responsibility, while the care of the crew should be his primary goal.

There are various approaches to wearing the responsibility of being the "old man" of the ship. The most notorious skipper ever to lead a crew was Captain William Bligh, master of the *Bounty* and the central villain of the best-selling story, *Mutiny On The Bounty*. Bligh was known in the British Admiralty as a brilliant young captain with a gift for navigation and attention to management and detail.

Among his men, Bligh was known for his strict discipline, his inflexibility, his harsh temper and his fondness for the lash.

During *Bounty*'s voyage to the South Pacific to collect breadfruit
for transplanting in the Caribbean, it was this second view which
very nearly brought Bligh down. In fact, because of his temper, his
inflexibility, his strict observation of every Admiralty detail, his men
put him over the side into a longboat with just enough provisions to
see him to the nearest islands.

Just about every modern sailor knows a Captain Bligh. Bloody-
minded, irrational, and with a hot and wild temper is not how most
skippers would choose to describe themselves. Yet too often novice
skippers assume a Captain Bligh pose as they attempt to overcome
their own uncertainties. Captain Bligh was not an effective leader of
a large ship, a large crew and an extended voyage. His manner and
personal style undid him. But it should be remembered, in any
discussion of Bligh, that after the men of *Bounty* had put their
skipper off in a longboat with several of his loyal crew, he completed
a nonstop, 3,000-mile voyage that ranks as one of the greatest small-
boat passages of all time.

If Bligh can be thought of as an example of how not to command
a crew and how not to run a ship, Captain James Cook can serve as a
fine model of how to be a successful skipper. Cook was a rarity in the
British navy of the late 18th century, for he had not achieved rank
by being born a gentleman but had risen through the ranks. Perhaps his humble beginnings as a boy deck hand on a Whitby collier
served him well as he gained ever more important commands.

Cook is noted as the man who explored the Pacific from east to
west and north to south, creating accurate maps, discovering new
landmasses and settling once and for all the long debate about the
phantom continent Terra Incognita—Antarctica. During three
model voyages, he managed to sail where none had sailed before,
yet he rarely lost a man and never put his crew or his ships in
danger. Cook traveled hopefully and peacefully, desiring only to
acquire knowledge of the Pacific and to open the world's largest
ocean to British commerce. It is ironic then that he ended his days
violently during a needless squabble with the Polynesian natives of
Hawaii.

While Cook's reputation rests largely on the success of his voyages and the charts he brought home with him, there is another aspect of the man that marks him as one of the great oceangoing commanders of men and ships. There is no doubt Cook was a remarkable navigator and an intrepid leader who always accomplished the tasks set out in his voyage plans. Yet he was also a skipper who put the safety and well-being of his crew and the safety of his ship ahead of a voyage's mission. He knew well, from his days as a young officer, that you can not complete a difficult or dangerous mission or voyage if your crew is unhealthy, unhappy or uncommitted. Cook saw to it that his crews were none of the three.

In the late 1700s, when Cook was making his long passages out from England to the Pacific and then remaining in the Pacific for months and years on end, the gravest threat to the success of a mission was not gales or uncharted reefs; it was scurvy. It was not uncommon during a protracted voyage for a captain to lose fully 30 percent of his working seamen to the disease. Cook, on the other hand, rarely lost a man to scurvy. A pioneer in nutrition, Cook carried all types of greens and fruit aboard on each of his voyages. The crew was unaccustomed to such fare and occasionally had to be forced to gag down spinach and limes. Yet the benefit of adding greens and fruit to the daily diet soon became apparent to those who sailed with Cook. It is no wonder that the captain never had trouble manning his vessels, no matter how long or uncertain his planned voyage.

Cook's loyalty to his men, his insistence on good health aboard his ship, his fairness as a leader, his vast experience and knowledge and his high personal standards in all his conduct with others made him one of the most highly regarded naval leaders of his day.

The qualities that made Cook a good leader can be transferred almost directly to the art of skippering a small ship manned by an amateur crew. The key to Cook's success, and to the success of many experienced cruising and racing skippers, is knowing that the well-being of the crew and the safety of the ship must come first. Only when a skipper is satisfied that he has done all within his power to achieve these ends should the importance of the voyage come into play.

Captain James Cook set a high standard. He is the epitome of the best an "old man" can be. Most recreational sailors will never match his commitment to detail, his insistence on careful and thoughtful planning, his commitment to his crew and his levelheadedness. But we can try.

THE SKIPPER AS MANAGER

Most of us who take to the sea with our friends and families have not had the benefit of a seafaring upbringing similar to that which spawned James Cook. Most of us have far more experience working in land-bound organizations—companies, schools, a profession or the public sector. For most of us, managing people, managing organizations and managing a plan into reality is the stuff of daily, workaday life.

In fact, the qualities of a good organizational leader—the natural manager—are the qualities that will turn even a novice sailor into a competent and capable skipper. Running a small ship is not dissimilar to running a small company—or, more to the point, a small nonprofit organization.

In a small organization, the success or failure of the enterprise depends almost exclusively on the founder or owner or resident leader. In most cases, all motivation for the organization, all long-range planning and all day-to-day guidance will flow from that one person, the skipper. The leader of a small organization must be able to improvise rapidly, must know the economic climate, must keep abreast of all technical and cultural changes that will affect the organization, must know how everything works around the shop and, most importantly, must be able to use his employees to the best of their abilities while making the most of their special talents.

A good skipper will do the same. Even though most of us take to the water and our boats for fun and recreation, and therefore do not wish to impose too drastic a structure upon those who sail with us, the responsibility of being skipper requires that we become the master of our world, the driving force in the enterprise of sailing, and the place where the buck always stops. Like a good manager, a good skipper will be able to make competent decisions rapidly, will know how to improvise, will be resourceful, will understand the weather and the sea, will be able to fix just about everything on-board and will know how to find the best in his crew and then put that best to work for the betterment of the ship and the passage.

Being a good skipper isn't easy, although the best skippers seem to wear their commands lightly and forge ahead with decisions and plans with little apparent effort and stress. It is easy for the rest of us to forget that such calm competence is the result of years of practice, of much trial and error and, naturally, of the many mistakes made along the way. The good skipper, like the good manager, learns quickly from watching others with more experience, by studying the literature of the game and by refusing to make the same mistake twice.

If any of the qualities of a good skipper are the most difficult to acquire, experience tells us that the three are: decision making, delegation of duties and knowing how to deal with crew. We'll cover these in the next sections.

DECISION MAKING ABOARD A BOAT

Captain Cook rose through the ranks of the British navy after first rising in the commercial coasting trade. No doubt the captain's humility and fairness as a leader stems in some degree from his experiences with harsh and whimsical skippers during his younger years. In his day, the skipper of a ship was a law unto himself, with the power to flog a man to within an inch of his life if he felt like it. Cook rarely, if ever, flogged a sailor. He didn't need to. His goal was to involve his officers, and through them his crew, in the workings of the ship, and through that involvement to foster a common purpose and a successful voyage.

There's not a lot of flogging on modern cruising boats. But listening to a high-strung novice tongue-lash his teenage children after having botched a landing at the gas dock, you realize that flogging does go on today, only the weapon has changed. Such a tongue-lashing is almost always the result of a mishap aboard the boat, which in turn was most likely the result of poor communications during a maneuver, which occurred because the skipper was indecisive and unable to issue clear, sensible commands. The kids caught it in the ear, but the skipper is the one feeling like an idiot.

Cook learned early, and most of us learn sooner or later, that to make a ship run smoothly, to make maneuvers trouble-free, to provide for the health and well-being of the crew, the skipper must be decisive. He must make his decisions in plenty of time, he must make the right decision (most of the time) and he must communicate that decision in plain language everyone understands. It doesn't sound too difficult, particularly for those who are accustomed to making dozens of decisions in their work. It's surprising, then, just how difficult decision making aboard a pleasure boat can be.

Racing boats are run like small naval vessels. There is no hint of democracy anywhere in the wind aboard highly competitive boats, nor should there be. The skipper, the tactician and the hired guns make the decisions. Everyone else sits on the rail and keeps his mouth shut.

On cruising boats, crewed by family members and friends, the process is a little different. The skipper's authority is not in any sense automatically accepted by the crew. In fact, if the crew is a family, the normal give and take, disputes, arguments and joking will all play a part in the decision-making process. Yet, even when the crew is a family, it is important for all on board to understand the need for a skipper and then to permit the skipper to make the final, much-considered decisions.

Failing to have one person at the center of the command structure will lead to disarray, poor decisions and ultimately to dangerous sailing.

Making decisions should not be a group activity in many instances. A ship cannot be run as a democracy, nor can efficient and safe decisions be taken in a town-meeting format. The buck has to stop somewhere and that somewhere is on the shoulders of the skipper. Yet, keeping Captain Cook's example in mind, decisions should always be taken with the crew's well-being and the safety of the ship foremost. It is important then that the crew be involved in the discussion of options, be asked for their thoughts, experience, and desires and that the skipper give weight and meaning to good ideas and good suggestions.

Experienced skippers will tell you that it is a rare crew that does not have something interesting to add to the mix of knowledge and experience already possessed by the skipper. Even if all the crew members add is a slightly different perspective on things, a joke or a tangential anecdote, the decision-making process will be enriched by the added spice. The well-being of the crew depends to a large extent upon a feeling of being involved in a meaningful way in the cruise or race. Once a skipper has taken advice, heard new ideas and then come to a decision, it is important for him to acknowledge those who contributed to the final decision. Personal acknowledgement is as valuable as a hot meal on a cold night at sea.

While a good skipper will be the master of his boat and will have learned how to operate and repair just about every item and system onboard, he should not always do everything himself. If a crew is brought along for the ride, they should be given chores to do, sheets to mind and tasks to perform. To make this possible, a skipper should be able to assess a crew member's strengths and weaknesses. There will be those who are comfortable with sails, rigging and sail trim. There will be those who enjoy having a wrench in one hand and a broken bit of pump or machinery in the other. There are those who are good at entertaining and those who have a talent for organizing hundreds of items in the boat's lockers. A skipper should try to pinpoint the strengths of those who sail with him and then devise ways to put those strengths to good use.

Equally as important as putting strengths to good use is finding ways to avoid the crew's weaknesses. Some weaknesses can be dealt with with humor. For example, if one crew member is always late for watch or when preparing meals, try putting that person in charge of the ship's schedule. If all the others are dependent upon the tardy one for their schedules, chances are they will make a point of reforming the sluggard. But there are many situations that can't be fixed. A sufferer from math anxiety shouldn't be put in charge of navigation; a sailor prone to seasickness shouldn't be the boat's sea cook; a clumsy or accident-prone sailor shouldn't be put in charge of the foredeck. A savvy skipper will make these determinations quickly at the beginning of a cruise and will only alter job allocations as behavior changes.

Although throughout this section we have been talking about a skipper and a crew, in most instances we are actually talking about a skipper and his friends and family. Considering strengths and weaknesses and allocating jobs on board accordingly in such company may seem a bit hard-boiled to those who have not done much sailing. Yet it is important to remember that even a close-knit family or a group of old friends wants and even demands a more formal group structure when sailing than it does when ashore. Failing to provide such a structure is both unsafe and unwise.

Once a skipper has sorted out his sailing companions and put everyone in charge of certain duties, enlisted their opinions and then taken the decisions that need to be taken, the last and most important part of the process is communicating the decisions to the crew. All too often people hear what they want to hear. After a simple discussion of a few present options and then a conclusion and decision by the skipper, there will always be one or more who missed the end and leave the discussion convinced their preferred course of action is the chosen one. The skipper must make sure everyone is clear about what is going on and why the decision was made.

There are several basic decision points on any extended sailing trip that can be useful in illustrating the decision-making process used by veteran skippers.

Scheduling. Never let a prearranged social or work schedule override a decision that should be based on weather conditions and seamanship. There is nothing in the world more pigheaded and potentially dangerous than slogging needlessly through deteriorating weather simply to show up at a cocktail party—even if that party is being thrown in honor of some VIP you want to impress.

Landfall. Never let the illusion of a safe harbor and a quiet night on the hook lead you into making a dangerous landfall in bad weather. A sound sailing craft is much safer hove-to at sea, weathering out a patch of wind and weather, than it is struggling to negotiate a tricky coast, a breaking harbor bar or a dangerous lee shore.

Action. Never let a safety-related task appear on a list of things to do tomorrow. If you perceive a problem with something—the rig, the anchor tackle, the pumps, the engineering—that directly affects the well-being of those onboard, fix it promptly. You may need that system working tonight, so tomorrow will be too late.

Abandon ship. Never leave a floating boat for a life raft. If the boat is sinking, prepare the raft and call for help. But continue to attempt to mend the leak until the decks are awash. Those who have spent time in life rafts will tell you that, while things might seem terrible aboard a disabled boat, aboard a raft things seem terribly final.

Leadership. Never let sensible seamanship and prudent leadership be compromised in a safety situation by the frailties of the crew. Panic, fear, seasickness, exhaustion and sudden phobias all can create dramatic diversions for the skipper. Yet, in bad weather, making decisions simply to allay some temporary unhappiness aboard while ignoring the dictates of wind, waves and seamanship will lead to further unhappiness and possibly a survival situation. Be firm. The safety of the boat and the well-being of all the crew—not just one unhappy camper—are the skipper's ultimate responsibilities.

Decision making can be simple or it can be arduous. The make-up of the crew, the weather confronted and the confidence of the skipper will all come into play in the decision-making process. There are still some Captain Blighs cruising our coasts and charging around the racecourses. Yet this is a vanishing breed, a breed that is rapidly developing skills at single-handing. There are more and more Captain Cooks piloting along the coasts today. These are the sailors who know that a committed, loyal, involved crew is always a happier crew and a happy crew always has the best time out on the water, no matter what the weather does.

THE ART OF DELEGATION

Unlike professional seamen or even delivery crews, most of us take to the sea purely for pleasure. We do not expect to face hardship and we do not expect to have to suffer the regimentation that hardship would require. Yet all sailors share the knowledge that one day we may find ourselves in a safety situation. We must be prepared, first, to enjoy the good weather we expect to find and, second, to be ready and competent in the unlikely event that we have to face adverse conditions.

To achieve both ends, it is important for a skipper to delegate as many responsibilities as possible to the crew members who are willing and able to handle them. Delegation of the responsibilities of running the boat will accomplish four very tangible results, all of which are good news for the skipper, good news for the crew and good for the safe running of the boat.

First, shared responsibility provides depth to the crew. While the skipper of a cruising or offshore racing boat may be able to do all tasks himself, there may be no backup for his knowledge if he fails to assign several diverse tasks to those who sail with him. Should the skipper who hoards his knowledge like a mysterious and arcane magic fall sick, fall overboard or otherwise become incapacitated, the crew that sailed so trustingly would be left unprepared to carry on a safe passage. By delegating, a skipper ensures that the crew can look after itself and can bring the boat home safely no matter what happens to him.

Second, delegating as much responsibility to the crew as is possible and practical allows those who sail with you to expand their knowledge, perfect their skills and discover new areas of strength and interest. Such involvement builds self-esteem, which in turn builds enthusiasm, teamwork and a sense of well-being. Crews that are involved in the actual workings of the boat will always be happier than those that are not.

Third, delegating specific tasks to the crew creates specialists who can stay on top of a few narrow fields of concern better than the skipper, who must remain a generalist. When things go wrong, the skipper will get better information about what is in fact wrong than if he was handling the responsibility alone. Moreover, if the skipper has to suddenly address one specific problem—a safety-related problem in particular—he can do so confident that others in the crew will be handling the ongoing functions of the boat.

Lastly, the act of delegating authority for specific tasks is the single most convincing way to establish a skipper's overall authority. The skipper defines the task to be done, establishes the way it is to be done and in what time frame, and then passes the execution along to one capable of handling it. In most cases the crew member will put the skipper's bidding into practice, while adding his own improvements and improvisations. If the skipper has a flexible and inquiring mind, he will embrace the crew member's individuality and learn from it. If he has a rigid, by-the-book mind, he will step in quickly to undo the innovations. In most cases, the crew member will be satisfied with either response, because his overriding concern is the fact that he was entrusted with an important task in the first place.

How to go about deciding which tasks to delegate and which to retain will depend to a great extent upon the skipper's own knowledge and skills and the competence and willingness of the crew. Yet it is safe to say that it is better in most cases to delegate more rather than less, to entrust the crew with greater rather than lesser responsibilities, and to monitor the activities of the crew instead of having to perform all tasks yourself.

Every skipper and crew will have to work out their own specific system for organizing the tasks to perform aboard a boat. To help those new to the process, below are several suggested ways to allocate jobs.

An Offshore-Delivery Crew

For passages of a thousand miles or more that have to be undertaken quickly and efficiently, a crew of three should be considered a minimum. In boats over forty feet long, a crew of five is even better. In a crew of three, you might want to allocate tasks in the following way:

Skipper. Overall responsibility; navigation; medical; communications; breakfast cook.

Next-best sailor. Backup skipper; engineering and electrical; backup navigation; sail trim; provisioning and provision stowage; cooking.

Third sailor. Helmsman; deck organization; cabin neatness; cooking and K.P.; music, games and entertainment; weather reports; main lookout.

IF YOU ARE sailing with five, the tasks of second and third sailors above can be divided among the extra two crew members. It should be noted that during fair-weather passages, a larger crew will increase the demands upon the galley and those in charge of provisions and cooking. And the entertainment officer will be under a lot of pressure to provide suitable diversions for those off watch.

A Couple

In Chapter 1 we discussed the importance of building teamwork between couples sailing without crew. While it is important for one member of the crew—usually the most experienced—to guide decision making and take on the role of skipper, it is unwise for anyone to assume "command." Men, in particular, who envision themselves the "captains" of their own ships and the masters of their destinies while relegating their spouses to the role of "second mate" deserve the mutiny they are sure to get.

The key to organizing tasks aboard is teamwork and flexibility. No one should have only scut work to do. No one should perform only interesting and engaging jobs. No one should do all the cooking or all the K.P. No one should be the sole user of the radio, the navigational instruments or the charts. It is folly to set up a formal captain-crew relationship, no matter how experienced the male might be and how inexperienced the female might be. Remember, if you choose to sail together, you should share the enjoyment and stimulation as well as the work.

That being the case, tasks should be organized by skill level, personal preference, by need and by inclination. Invariably, certain unsavory jobs will be left unclaimed. These should be divided as fairly as possible, taking into account the need for both sailors to be as well-rounded, as capable of singlehanding as possible.

The Sailing Family

No other sailing crew is more common and more difficult to pin down than a family that sails together. While a conventional family unit often tends to allocate tasks in somewhat traditional ways on land and will carry that pattern over to life aboard a boat, such a formula is not necessarily the best approach. Sailing together is not like sharing a house. Sailing requires teamwork, involvement and a sharing of responsibilities far more than does life ashore. At sea, everyone's safety depends upon all of the crew—whether that crew is comprised of salty men or small children.

Organizing a family unit into a sailing crew is not an easy task. But those who have been successful at it have demonstrated the benefits of including all family members in the workings of the boat, in decisions, in the work and play of sailing. Children, who may be overwhelmed by the idea of sailing a large sailboat themselves, can easily grasp lesser, specific tasks over which they are expected to have control—tailing jib sheets, adjusting the traveler, mixing up cool drinks and so on.

Delegation of duties is more important within a family unit afloat than it is ashore. If the husband and wife intend to be as safety conscious as possible, then both must be able to handle their boat alone or with the help of the children. If one adult goes over the side, the remaining crew must be able to perform the recovery maneuvers.

In addition, if the children are to enjoy sailing, if they are going to feel committed to the time on the water, the confines of the boat and the long hours of sailing that can become boring, then they must have special tasks that belong to them. Such tasks should be small enough to be handled without frustration, but important enough to the well-being of the crew to make them significant in the child's own eyes. Taking care of music, organizing games for all to play, being in charge of the binoculars and the bird and sea mammal books, running the fishing tackle are all jobs that can occupy a child's attention and make him feel involved with the ongoing process of sailing the boat.

Other tasks children can perform with a degree of competence and satisfaction include: flaking anchor chain in the chain locker as it comes over the windlass; pumping the bilge daily or as needed; trimming smaller sails, such as a mizzen or staysail; monitoring the radio for current weather broadcasts; acting as a lookout in poor weather; assisting in the galley; monitoring the course for the helmsman and even temporary helmsman; and acting as the skipper of the dinghy.

A family is the best crew for cruising, for within a family there is a built-in sense of teamwork. If this sense can be translated into real action, into specific tasks, then a family can enjoy many hours, days and weeks together on the water.

A CREW'S BILL OF RIGHTS

Sailing as a family, as a couple, or with a few friends is normally a happy endeavor. For the most part the weather will be fine, the sea will not kick up and trouble will not interfere. Sailors who have prepared themselves well for their time on the water have few safety emergencies and a small chance of something going drastically wrong.

However, the ultimate responsibility for all going smoothly on any sailing boat lies with the skipper. Foremost of those responsibilities is to bring his crew—spouse, family and friends—home again safely. It is not only the skipper's obligation to do so, it is the crew's right to sail with a skipper who takes his responsibility seriously.

To bring the skipper's responsibilities into focus, the following Crew's Bill of Rights may prove useful, for the list itemizes the planning, preparation and practice that the skipper must embrace if he is to run a safe, well-found boat.

THE CREW OF every sailing boat embarking on open water has the following rights, which must be honored by every skipper:

To sail in safe seasons and in safe areas
To sail in a well-found boat
To be prepared and equipped for any contingency
To be warm, dry and well fed
To know the rules and traditions of the sea
To know boat handling well enough to overcome difficulties
To be prepared for heavy weather
To be able to recover a man overboard
To be able to survive catastrophic damage to the mother ship

Any skipper planning to take or dreaming of taking a boat and crew onto open water, along a coast or across an ocean must be able to meet the basic rights of the crew. Failing to meet any of the rights above not only can spell a sailor's failure as a skipper, it can also mean the needless loss of an innocent life. It is the crew's right to survive. It is the skipper's obligation to see that they do.

CONCLUSION

After 25 years of sailing, after some 30,000 miles of offshore and coastal racing and cruising, after owning a string of boats from 23 to 43 feet, I am still struck by the awesome responsibility of taking command of a boat and crew and putting to sea.

Self-reliance, freedom, peace, adventure—these are the qualities we seek in our time on the water. Sailing, whether cruising along a coastline or striking out across an ocean, is a unique pastime, for it offers all who take part a rich and engaging experience.

Yet, unlike most other pastimes, the enjoyment of sailing is ineluctably entwined with a conscientious attitude toward safety. You and your crew can die out there. It is up to you, up to the skipper of the boat, up to the crew to run a tight ship that is well prepared for the rigors as well as the pleasures of the sea.

INDEX